Twelve Gifts of Christmas

From Our Heavenly Father

STUDY   GUIDE

Stanley Holstein

Twelve Gifts of Christmas From Our Heavenly Father Study Guide

Copyright © 2022 Stanley Holstein.

All rights reserved. No portion of this book may be reproduced, stored in a retrieval system, or transmitted in any form or by any means—electronic, mechanical, photocopy, recording, scanning, or other—except for brief quotations in critical reviews or articles, without the prior written permission of the publisher.

Published by SLH Publishing; P.O. Box 177, Bluffton, OH 45817;

Website: https://hopethroughthetruth.com.

Words in brackets [ ] have been added by the author for clarification.

All Scripture quotations, unless otherwise indicated, are taken from the Holy Bible, New International Version®, NIV®. Copyright ©1973, 1978, 1984, 2011 by Biblica, Inc.® Used by permission of Zondervan. All rights reserved worldwide; www.zondervan.com. The "NIV" and "New International Version" are trademarks registered in the United States Patent and Trademark Office by Biblica, Inc.®

Scripture quotations marked (ESV), taken from the ESV® Bible (The Holy Bible, English Standard Version®) copyright © 2001 by Crossway Bibles, a publishing ministry of Good News Publishers, are used by permission. All rights reserved. The "ESV" and "English Standard Version" are registered trademarks of Good News Publishers.

Scripture quotations marked (KJV), taken from The Holy Bible: King James Version; Electronic Edition of the 1900 Authorized Version. Bellingham, WA: Logos Research Systems, Inc., 2009; are used by permission.

Quotations taken from *Twelve Gifts of Christmas From Our Heavenly Father*, Stanley Holstein, copyright © 2021, are used by permission of SLH Publishing, P.O. Box 177, Bluffton, OH 45817; https://hopethroughthetruth.com.

Quotations taken from *Hope Through the Truth Standing in the Gap in America*, Stanley Holstein, copyright © 2020, are used by permission of SLH Publishing, P.O. Box 177, Bluffton, OH 45817; https://hopethroughthetruth.com.

Any websites, phone numbers, or company or product information printed in this book are offered as a resource and are not intended in any way to be or to imply an endorsement by the publisher; nor does the publisher vouch for the existence, content, or services of these sites, phone numbers, companies, or products.

Book cover design and interior book formatting by 100 Covers.

A very special thanks to the editors, Don Boehm and Kathy Boehm; whose teaching experience and knowledge of the Bible have made this guide more organized, reader-friendly, and scripturally accurate.

ISBN 978-1-7360865-7-5 (eBook)
ISBN 978-1-7360865-6-8 (paperback)

Printed in the United States of America.

Table of Contents

Preface 1
Introduction 3
Lesson 1: Jesus Christ – The First Gift of Christmas 5
Lesson 2: Grace – The Gift of God's Plan 19
Lesson 3: Life – A Daily Gift from God 33
Lesson 4: Being Chosen by God Is His Gift 47
Lesson 5: Our Faith in God Comes From Him 61
Lesson 6: The Desire to Live for God Is His Gift 75
Lesson 7: The Holy Spirit – God's Power in Us 89
Lesson 8: The Fruit of the Holy Spirit – God Producing in Us .. 103
Lesson 9: The Word of God – His Gift of Revelation 117
Lesson 10: Adopted by God – His Gift to Spiritual Orphans ... 131
Lesson 11: A Living Hope – God's Gift of Encouragement 145
Lesson 12: Eternal Life – The Final Gift of Christmas 159
Small Group Leader's Guide 173
Notes 177

Preface

The lessons in this study relate to information contained in the book *Twelve Gifts of Christmas From Our Heavenly Father*. However, you don't need that book to use this study guide. Any statements such as "the author says," "the author writes," "the author has written elsewhere," or "in his book;" are referring to portions of text taken directly from that book.

God the Father offers many gifts to those who love him. This study addresses twelve of those, beginning with the birth of God's Son, Jesus Christ, the Messiah. Each topic is discussed in detail as portrayed in the Holy Bible; culminating with the final gift, eternal life through faith in Jesus Christ as Lord and Savior. My hope is, through this study, we will truly ponder and realize the incomprehensible extravagance of each gift our heavenly Father has given us. May we consider how each present enables us to live life to the full on Earth while preparing us for a glorious eternity.

To dwell on such matters is so important since I, as a believer, still have a powerful force with which I must reckon every day; my self-centered nature. Far too often, I view God's plan of salvation from a "me" perspective. *I* chose to accept Jesus Christ as Lord and Savior.

I exhibited the faith to believe. *I . . . I . . . I.* Sometimes, I think it's all about me.

As we delve into Scripture, we will recall, or maybe even realize for the first time, what God says about the origin of faith to believe in Jesus Christ, the desire to live a godly life, and other eternal matters. Those who have studied the Bible will likely have read every verse and discussed every topic we will cover here. Yet, in coal-miners' parlance, as we "dig" into the Word of God regarding these fundamental matters, sincerely desiring to be enlightened by the Holy Spirit; he will lead us to "nuggets" of wisdom worth far more than gold.

No matter how much biblical wisdom we have acquired, returning to the basics of Scripture is always profitable. As Peter wrote to the first century believers:

> "So, I will always remind you of these things, even though you know them and are firmly established in the truth you now have.. . . And I will make every effort to see that after my departure you will always be able to remember these things" (2 Peter 1:12, 15).

Near the end of this study a personal question will be posed regarding our salvation; "At the moment of my repentance, what did I bring to the foot of the cross?" That was the most illuminating question for me during the course of this study. Hopefully, you will keep this question in the back of your mind as you open each of the twelve gifts. May God bless you richly for your efforts in this endeavor.

Introduction

I love the Christmas holiday season. It has produced so many fond memories for me. Mom and Dad loved Jesus, and this time of year was all about his birth. This season was special to me for other reasons. There was no school. Bedtime curfews were loosened and snack times became more plentiful. Best of all, I knew presents were coming soon. There was a sense of excitement and expectation in the air for me. How could it get any better?

My brother Tim recalled, "We always had good Christmases. Mom and Dad made sure of it. As a kid, I never thought about the joy it brought them to see the sheer delight they created for their children." Neither did I. Every parent I know wants to provide the basic care that their children need to survive. But their desire goes much further. They also want their children to succeed in life in every possible way. Parents want to give their children every good gift that will benefit them. God, our heavenly Father, wants to give us every good and perfect gift because he loves us. The desire of his heart is to be our father and for us to be his children, his loving family.

As a child, I would always awaken early on Christmas morning filled with excitement. I would scurry down the steps into the living room to behold the tree, with lights ablaze and gifts stuffed underneath. It was with great anticipation, and no small amount of frustration, that I waited for the rest of the family to arrive, so we could tear into the presents.

When I was a youngster, Christmas was all about receiving gifts. As an adult, this holiday became about me giving gifts to loved ones. As a Christian adult, I have heard many comments regarding how Christmas has become commercialized; has lost its true meaning as a celebration of the birth of Jesus Christ. I share these opinions. However, if anyone would ask me, "For a Christian, is Christmas really about gifts?" My response would be, "Yes, absolutely." But the gifts to which I would be referring are spiritual rather than material. To be sure, God has given, and continues to give, me many earthly blessings: a good job, the opportunity to live to retirement, good health, and a nice home, to mention just a few. Yet, the eternal gifts I have received are far more precious.

As we engage in this study, travel back in time with me to one of your early Christmas mornings; infused with that same child-like exuberance. However, this time, let's view the brightly wrapped packages under the tree with spiritual eyes and envision the giver as God the Father. May we relish each precious present as we open *Twelve Gifts of Christmas From our Heavenly Father*.

Lesson 1

Jesus Christ – The First Gift of Christmas

But the gift is not like the trespass. For if the many died by the trespass of the one man, how much more did God's grace and the gift that came by the grace of the one man, Jesus Christ, overflow to the many! (Romans 5:15)

On the first day of Christmas my true love gave to me, a Savior, my source of liberty.

Observation

Twelve Gifts of Christmas From Our Heavenly Father, chapters 1 through 3, discuss the origin and development of the Christmas holiday. They also identify Jesus Christ as the first gift of Christmas. The author has stated:

> "My memories of the Christmas season include wonderful times of family gatherings, plentiful food, and ample presents. Though my childhood is long gone, those early memories remain vivid. I clearly remember the excitement and anticipation of opening presents. However, that excitement didn't last long after Christmas morning had passed. I appreciated some gifts more than others. I certainly enjoyed the toy dump truck far longer than the sweater I received."[1]

What were some of your best memories of Christmas as a child? What were some of your best memories of Christmas as an adult? How, if at all, has becoming a Christian altered your view of Christmas?

Contemplation

(Suggested reading – Matthew 7:9-11; 1 Corinthians 12:4; James 1:17)

1. As a Christian, do you believe Christmas is about gifts? Why or why not?

_____
_____
_____
_____
_____

(Suggested reading – Matthew 2:1-2 & 9:27; John 6:42)

2. By what worldly names or titles was Jesus known during his time on Earth?

(Suggested reading – Matthew 1:23; Luke 2:11; John 5:25)

3. By what heavenly names or titles was Jesus known during his time on Earth?

(Suggested reading – Matthew 27:50; Luke 2:4-7; Hebrews 2:17)

4. What scriptural evidence indicates Jesus was human?

(Suggested reading – John 1:1 & 18; Philippians 2:5-8; Colossians 1:15-19)

5. What scriptural evidence indicates Jesus is divine?

_____

_____

_____

_____

_____

(Suggested reading – Isaiah 9:6; John 4:10; Romans 5:15-17)

6. Does the Bible describe Jesus Christ as a gift to humanity?

_____

_____

_____

_____

_____

Inspiration

George C. Lorimer (1838 – 1904), born in Edinburgh, Scotland, came to the United States in 1856, attended college, and became a Baptist minister pastoring churches in Kentucky, New York, Illinois, and Massachusetts. In his book, *The Galilean*, he writes:

"He [John] is mystical, transcendental, theological. His Christ is from the first [the] Divine incarnation, concerning whom it is more important to know that he is the Son of God than that he is the Son of Mary. He is a being on the Earth, but not of the Earth, moving about in heavenly fellowships, angels descending and ascending on him, and voices of the Eternal guiding and comforting him. The servant of Mark's Gospel that rises to kingship in Matthew's, and the king of Matthew's Gospel that attains to the higher rank of brother in Luke's, here transcends all human limitations, and appears in alliance with God."[2]

"To her [the church] Jesus is, as Irenaeus expresses it, "Born and unborn, God in flesh, life in death, born of Mary, born of God." As Bishop Hopkins has it, she [the church] declares, "In him omnipotence became weak, eternity mortal, innocence itself guilty, God man, the Creator a creature, the Maker of all his own workmanship, a King without regalia, God without the thunder; a child, without the heart for play.. . ."

Yes, according to the Inspired Book, Jesus is the meeting place of two worlds—the human world and the divine. The essence of all being centers in him. Godhood and manhood are united in him forever. Limitless ubiquity [being everywhere] enshrines itself in limitable space, measureless eternity enfolds itself in measurable time, incomprehensible infinity clothes itself with comprehensible finitude [having limits or bounds]. The inscrutable [impossible to understand] becomes the familiar, the unknown the known, the invisible the visible, the spiritual the incarnate, and the total result is Jesus of Nazareth."[3]

Response

(Suggested reading – Matthew 1:21 & 2:22-23; Mark 1:23-24; John 19:19-20)

7. What significance, if any, do you attach to the name "Jesus of Nazareth"?

_____

_____

_____

_____

Preface to question 8 – The Greek word for "Christ" and the Hebrew word for "Messiah" have the same meaning; "anointed." According to the *Illustrated Bible Dictionary*:

> Christ—meaning anointed, is the Greek translation of the Hebrew word rendered "Messiah," the official title of our Lord.. . . It denotes that he was anointed or consecrated to his great redemptive work as Prophet, Priest, and King of his people.. . . Jesus the Christ is Jesus the Great Deliverer, the Anointed One, the Savior of men. This name denotes that Jesus was divinely appointed, commissioned, and accredited as the Savior of men.[4]
>
> Messiah—(Hebrew mashiah) meaning anointed, is rendered "Christos." Thus priests, prophets, and kings were anointed with oil, and so consecrated to their respective offices. The

great Messiah is anointed "above his fellows;" i.e., he embraces in himself all the three offices.. . . Jesus of Nazareth is the Messiah, the great Deliverer who was to come.[5]

(Suggested reading – Daniel 9:21-26; Isaiah 61:1-2; Luke 4:16-21; 1 John 2:20, 27)

8. What significance, if any, do you attach to the names "Christ" and "Messiah"?

(Suggested reading – Matthew 9:6, 14:32-33 & 26:64; Mark 3:11; Luke 1:35; John 3:13)

9. Compare and contrast two titles of Jesus; "Son of Man" and "Son of God."

Preface to question 10 – An abbreviated history of the divided Kingdom of Israel is provided here to show some factors prompting the Israelites, in the thousand years before Christ, to increasingly anticipate the "one who is to come."

- God promised David, the second king of the united Kingdom of Israel [@ 1005–965 BC], "Your throne will be established forever" (2 Samuel 7:16).
- During the reign of Rehoboam, the grandson of David through Solomon; the united Kingdom of Israel was divided into two kingdoms; Judah [Southern Kingdom] and Israel [Northern Kingdom]. Rehoboam remained king of Judah [Southern Kingdom] and Jeroboam became king of Israel [Northern Kingdom] (1 Kings 12:1, 12-21).
- Hoshea, [the last king of Israel, (Northern Kingdom) @ 732–721 BC], rebelled against Shalmaneser king of Assyria. Sometime around 721 BC, the Assyrians captured Samaria and deported many Israelites to Assyria [@ 722 BC] (2 Kings 17:1, 4-6).
- This marked the end of the Northern Kingdom of Israel.
- Zedekiah, [the last king of Judah, Southern Kingdom], was overthrown by the Babylonians under Nebuchadnezzar; resulting in deportations of Judah's people [@ 587 BC] to Babylon (2 Kings 24:18) (2 Kings 25:1, 2, 5 & 11-12).
- This marked the end of the Southern Kingdom.
- During the eighth through the sixth centuries BC, prophets foretold the "one who is to come." From the earlier to the later writings, these mouthpieces of God said:
    - "One who will be ruler over Israel.. . . He will stand and shepherd his flock in the strength of the Lord, in the majesty of the name of the Lord his God.. . . His greatness will reach to the ends of the earth" (Micah 5:2, 4).

- "I will raise up . . . a righteous Branch, a King. . . . He will be called: The Lord Our Righteous Savior" (Jeremiah 23:5-6).
- "The Anointed One, the ruler, comes.. . . It [Jerusalem] will be rebuilt.. . . The Anointed One will be put to death and will have nothing" (Daniel 9:25–26).

(Suggested reading – Matthew 11:2-3; John 11:27; Acts 19:4)

10. What passages are there in Scripture, if any, indicating the first century Israelites were looking for an "anointed one" or "one who is to come?"

_____
_____
_____
_____
_____

(Suggested reading – Matthew 13:13-15; Luke 23:3; John 6:14-15, 12:12-15 & 18:36)

11. Why did the overwhelming majority of those who were looking for the "one who is to come" reject Jesus's identity and message?

_____
_____
_____
_____
_____

(Suggested reading – same as for questions 4 and 5)

12. So, was Jesus Christ fully human only; fully divine only; part human and part divine; or fully human as well as fully divine? How did you make your determination from the Bible?

Practical Points to Consider

Unanswered or Additional Relevant Questions

Prayer

Heavenly Father, I thank you that you sent Jesus Christ from heaven to Earth, born of a woman, to introduce yourself to us and give us your gospel message. Lord, my limited mind cannot truly comprehend fully human and fully divine at the same time in one person. I accept your Word as truth, though I don't understand it completely. Help me to realize everything you intended me to know about you and your Son, Jesus. Lead me into a closer relationship with you and your Son as I study your Word. In Jesus's name I pray. Amen.

Journaling

Jesus Christ – The First Gift of Christmas

Lesson 2
Grace – The Gift of God's Plan

For it is by grace you have been saved, through faith—and this is not from yourselves, it is the gift of God. (Ephesians 2:8)

On the second day of Christmas my true love gave to me, his plan from sin and death to set me free.

Observation

Twelve Gifts of Christmas, chapter 4, discusses God's grace as his gift to us. That word, grace, is used so many different ways in the English language. *Chambers' Dictionary* defines grace as "easy elegance in form or manner, to adorn or mark with favor, embellishment, friendship, pardon, a ceremonious title, a short prayer at meals, or the undeserved mercy of God."[1]

When we focus on the biblical definition of grace, it can be described in different ways. *The Church Cyclopaedia* speaks of grace as a "word that originally meant the free gift, favor, or benefit.. . . It is one of the most important of all the terms used, for the grace of our Lord, Jesus Christ, the free gift he bestows of everlasting life, the free gift of the Holy Spirit and all the blessings that attend his presence, the favors and benefits that the practice of the Christian virtues procures in our daily life, are all comprehended under that one all-embracing word."[2]

Robert N. McKaig was a nineteenth-century minister from Indiana. In his book, *The Life and Times of the Holy Spirit*, he writes: "We . . . observe how the truth and grace of God are further revealed to man.. . . It was prophesied that he would make a short work upon the Earth. The truth manifested . . . is the birth of Christ, his words and works; his death, resurrection, and ascension. The grace revealed is the grace of pardon for the penitents [feeling sorrow or regret for having done wrong], the grace of peace with God through our Lord Jesus Christ to the believer. The grace of freedom from the condemnation of sin."[3]

The author has stated, "My daughter, Hannah, used to ask me what I wanted for Christmas. My standard reply was, "I could use a pair of black dress socks" or some other equally lame response. While I'm certain my answers drove her crazy, she would always diligently search for something I would enjoy; and was always quite successful. She seems to have a knack for choosing the perfect gift for me.

Christmas morning, 2012, was no exception as I opened my presents. One was a book with an inscription on the first page that read, "Dad, while I may have a hard time finding gifts for you; I give you this as a reminder of God's greatest gift to us. I hope you enjoy. Love, Hannah." The book was Max Lucado's, *Grace – More Than We Deserve – Greater Than We Imagine*. With five small words, Hannah simply and succinctly captured the essence of grace, "God's greatest gift to us."[4]

Contemplation

(Suggested reading – Romans 3:23-25; Galatians 2:16, 20 & 21; Ephesians 2:8-9)

1. How would you define God's grace? Is it limited to his plan of salvation?

(Suggested reading – John 3:17 & 6:40; 1 Timothy 2:3-6; 2 Peter 3:9)

2. What is God's desire for humanity regarding salvation?

(Suggested reading – Genesis 6:18, 8:18-22, & 15:4-10; Exodus 12:4-7, 12 & 13, 30:10)

3. What is the relationship, if any, between a covenant with God and the shedding of blood? If you can, give examples.

(Suggested reading – Leviticus 17:11; Hebrews 9:11-15 & 22)

4. How, if at all, do the sacrifices in the Old Testament relate to or foreshadow the sacrifice of Jesus Christ?

(Suggested reading – Genesis 14:18; Hebrews 7:1-3 & 10)

5. What was the first priesthood established in the Old Testament?

Preface to question 6 – Hebrews 7:11 asks, "If perfection could have been attained through the Levitical priesthood—and indeed the law given to the people established that priesthood—why was there still need for another priest to come, one in the order of Melchizedek, not in the order of Aaron?"

(Suggested reading – Hebrews 5:1-3; 7:11-16 & 20-27; 10:11-12; 1 John 3:5)

6. What are the major differences between these two priesthoods?

_____

_____

_____

_____

Inspiration

As believers, we may sometimes tend to focus on New Testament passages and teachings. This is logical since we are the church, members of the body of Christ, which was established in the New Testament. However, it is important to remember that the Old Testament is critical to every believer. The history contained in the first books of the Bible describes the requirements for a relationship to exist between God and humanity.

Furthermore, the law is the foundation upon which God's grace is built. The calling of the Israelite nation to be set apart, the Levitical priesthood with its sacrificial system, the old covenant which we know as Mosaic law, and many of the people in the Old Testament; point to the coming Messiah. He is the one who was to come, the sacrificial Lamb of God; through whom God's grace provides the pathway to restore humanity's relationship with our heavenly Father.

Alexander Patterson, a twentieth-century Presbyterian minister in Illinois, refers to the Old Testament foreshadowing the coming Christ. In his book, *The Greater Life and Work of Christ*, he writes:

"In the Old Testament . . . there are certain specifically named persons who are appointed to represent Christ as types. Adam was the first, representing Christ as the head of the race. Melchizedek was the type of the priesthood of Christ, Moses with Joshua a type of his prophetic office, David with Solomon types of the Christ in his kingship as Son of David to Israel.. . .

Jonah was a type of his burial. Israel as a nation . . . was a Messiah among the nations.. . . The Old Testament . . . was written in symbols. These are seen from the tree of life down through the long line of appointed types of things natural or artificial, all the articles and ceremonies of the tabernacle and the temple, and the entire ritual of worship.. . .

The coming Christ was fully revealed.. . . Israel seemed to gradually come to understand the truth as to the coming.. . . To Abraham the coming Christ was the longed-for Seed; to Jacob a deliverer; to Moses a revelation of glory; to David an heir.. . . Yet Christ was not fully foreseen even by the utterers of the prophecies.. . . Most of the predictions of the Messiah came in their declining days, and they saw what they most desired, a Deliverer coming in glory."[5]

Response

(Suggested reading – Luke 22:20; Romans 3:20; Hebrews 7:18-19; 9:15 & 10:1-4; James 2:10)

7. What was the purpose of the old covenant (the law, Mosaic law) and what is the purpose of the new covenant (grace)?

_____

_____

_____

_____

_____

_____

(Suggested reading – Romans 8:2; Colossians 2:17; Hebrews 8:13, 9:1 & 9-14, 10:1)

8. Aside from their purposes, what are the major differences between the old covenant and the new covenant?

_____

_____

_____

_____

_____

_____

(Suggested reading – John 3:14-18; Acts 2:37-39 & 3:19; Romans 10:9-10)

9. The question, "What must I do to be saved or inherit eternal life?" or some close variation of it, is posed in Scripture at least four times. How would you respond to such a question?

(Suggested reading – Romans 8:3-4; Hebrews 4:15; 1 Timothy 3:16)

10. Did God's law require Jesus to come to Earth as a human and die? If so, which laws?

Preface to question 11 – Jesus makes a unique claim in John 14:6 saying, "I am the way and the truth and the life. No one comes to the Father except through me." Not "one of many ways" but "the way;" singular.

(Suggested reading – John 10:17-18; Acts 4:12; 1 Peter 2:24; Revelation 5:3-9)

11. In what way or ways is Jesus Christ unique not only on Earth, but in heaven as well?

(Suggested reading – Matthew 7:21-23 & 15:7-9; John 14:23-24; Acts 20:22-24)

12. Can Jesus Christ be your Savior without being the Lord of your life? Why or why not?

Practical Points to Consider

Unanswered or Additional Relevant Questions

Prayer

Heavenly Father, thank you for your love, mercy, and grace. Thank you for continually encouraging me to believe in your Son. Thank you for the life lessons you gave me in the Old Testament and the many examples of institutions and people who point to the Messiah, the one who was to come. Help me to realize how much I can see the Christ in both the Old and New Testaments as I read and study about your grace extended to me. In Jesus's name I pray. Amen.

Journaling

Twelve Gifts of Christmas - From Our Heavenly Father - Study Guide

Lesson 3
Life – A Daily Gift from God

And he is not served by human hands, as if he needed anything. Rather, he himself gives everyone life and breath and everything else. (Acts 17:25)

On the third day of Christmas my true love gave to me, the breath of life so I could come to be.

Observation

Twelve Gifts of Christmas, chapter 5, discusses life as God's gift to us. The author has stated:

> "Recently, the breath of life became a focus of attention worldwide. COVID-19, a virus that causes a respiratory infection and many times impedes proper breathing, has swept throughout the world. As a result, we have all learned more than we ever wanted to know about ventilators and other makeshift breathing machines. We now understand how few we had, how they are made, and how many we may need. I took breathing for granted until mine was interrupted. But it's not only illness, disease, or injury that may impair or stop a person's ability to breathe.
>
> I am convinced that no human is conceived, born, or continues to live without permission from God Almighty. I need to continually recognize that even my breath is not my own. If you think you control your breathing, try this experiment. Hold your breath until you become unconscious. You can't do it, can you? When I think about the "breath of life," God breathing life into Adam always comes to mind. Yet rarely do I consider the fact that God may decide to take away my breath next year, next month, or in the next minute."[1]

To those God has given life; he also wants them to be satisfied with their time on Earth. Solomon wrote:

- Moreover, when God gives someone wealth and possessions, and the ability to enjoy them, to accept their lot and be happy in their toil—this is a gift of God (Ecclesiastes 5:19).

- So, I saw that there is nothing better for a person than to enjoy their work, because that is their lot (Ecclesiastes 3:22).

God wants humanity not only to enjoy life on Earth, but to realize who he is through the universe and glorify him. Michael J. Carlowicz, managing editor of the NASA Earth Observatory and one of the authors of the book *Earth*, captures the essence of the awe our planet can inspire. The book itself is a pictorial display of our planet's majestic scenery as seen from space. In the foreword of this book, he states,

> "From its origins, NASA has studied our planet in novel ways, using ingenious tools to study physical processes at work . . . examining the cycles and processes—the water cycle, the carbon cycle, ocean circulation, the movement of heat—that interact and influence each other in a complex, dynamic dance across seasons and decades.. . .
>
> For all of the dynamism and detail we can observe from orbit, sometimes it is worth stepping back and simply admiring Earth. It is a beautiful, awe-inspiring place, and it is the only world most of us will ever know.. . . The pages of this book . . . tell a story of a . . . planet where there is always something new to see. They tell a story of land, wind, water, ice, and air as they can only be viewed from above. They show us that no matter what the human mind can imagine, no matter what the artist can conceive, there are few things more fantastic and inspiring than the world as it already is. The truth of our planet is just as compelling as any fiction."[2]

Contemplation

(Suggested reading – Genesis 2:7; Job 12:10; Psalm 104:29; Isaiah 42:5; Revelation 11:11)

1. The phrase "breath of life" occurs six times in the NIV and seven times in the ESV Bible. Who is its originator? What does this phrase mean to you?

___

(Suggested reading – Job 10:10-11; Psalm 139:13-15; Ecclesiastes 11:5)

2. When you study how the human body functions; what "miracles," if any, do you see?

3. Do you consider the human body to be fragile or resilient? Why?

4. How is our planet uniquely (as far as we know) designed to support human life?

(Suggested reading – Genesis 2:1 & 15:5; Jeremiah 33:22)

5. What do we know (or believe) regarding the number of stars and galaxies and the size of our universe?

(Suggested reading – Psalm 8:1-4 & 19:1-4; Isaiah 45:12; Romans 1:18-21)

6. Do other planets (excluding our moon), stars (excluding our Sun), and galaxies; impact life on Earth? If yes, how? If not, for what purpose or purposes did God create them?

_____

_____

_____

_____

Inspiration

The Bible says, "I know that there is nothing better for people than to be happy and to do good while they live. That each of them may eat and drink, and find satisfaction in all their toil—this is the gift of God" (Ecclesiastes 3:12–13).

Not only did God give us gifts of life, an exquisitely beautiful nurturing home, and spectacular heavens surrounding us; he also gave us an eternal purpose to achieve while living on Earth. Scripture tells us:

> For God did not call us to be impure, but to live a holy life
> (1 Thessalonians 4:7).

This can only be achieved by our most dedicated efforts through the power of the indwelling Holy Spirit. The Bible says:

> "Therefore, if anyone is in Christ, the new creation has come:
> The old has gone, the new is here" (2 Corinthians 5:17).

This new creation, "in Christ," is radically different from the "old self," as we point others to the Lord Jesus Christ and give glory to God in everything we do. By the way, did you know the NIV Bible contains the phrase "in Christ" more than 85 times in the New Testament? I believe the regenerated human soul is the greatest work in God's creation.

William Paley (1743–1805) was an Anglican priest, Archdeacon of Carlisle in England, and an author of influential works on Christianity. In his book, *A View of the Evidences of Christianity*, he discusses the change in a saved soul writing:

> "We are not, perhaps, at liberty to take for granted that the lives of the preachers of Christianity were as perfect as their lessons. But we are entitled to contend, that the observable part of their behavior must have agreed in a great measure with the duties which they taught. There was, therefore (which is all that we assert), a course of life pursued by them, different from that which they led before."[3]

James B. Walker (1805–1887) was an American minister who established a home for orphans in Mansfield, Ohio. In his book, *The Doctrine of the Holy Spirit*, he writes about our high calling:

> "Now the apostles understood the necessity of the incarnation in this respect. Christ's character, manifested by his life, was the model into which they sought to mold humanity. He was 'the mark of the prize of the high calling' [Philippians 3:14 KJV] to which they struggled to attain, while they invited others to the same endeavor.. . . That is, Christ assumed a sanctified humanity in order that his followers might be sanctified by conformity to his image.. . . They were, by assimilation to his life and spirit, raised from the sphere of the earthly, mortal, Adamic species, into the sphere of a new spiritual life, of which Christ was himself the head and elder brother."[4]

"When comparing themselves with Christ, all Christians will see imperfection in their obedience—but they will be conscious of an obedient spirit, trust in Christ's mercy, and this is the true Christian consciousness in light or darkness."[5]

"The will of God, and not his own will, is the law of life with the believer. But while the law is obeyed as a rule of duty, that law is likewise an expression of the will and heart of his divine benefactor. Christian life is not, therefore, the service of duty under the impulse of conscience alone. The impulse of love is united with the element of conscience."[6]

Response

(Suggested reading – Genesis 1:26; Matthew 6:26; John 4:7-14; 6:26-27 & 32-35; Romans 5:8)

7. Is every human valuable to God? What Bible verses support your response?

(Suggested reading – Matthew 5:16; Acts 17:26-27; Ephesians 4:22-24)

8. For what purpose or purposes did God create humans?

(Suggested reading – 1 Corinthians 10:31; Colossians 3:17; 1 Peter 1:15 & 4:11)

9. If you were to combine all of the aforementioned purposes of humanity into one sentence to form a Christian's mission statement, what would that statement say?

(Suggested reading – Genesis 1:26 & 2:15; Psalm 8:6-8)

10. What responsibility if any, do we have to God regarding our planet?

(Suggested reading – Matthew 7:13-14 & 22:14; Luke 13:23-24)

11. How many humans, of all those ever conceived, do you believe will spend eternity with our triune God? What scriptural basis supports your conclusion?

(Suggested reading – Matthew 28:19-20; Luke 10:2; Ephesians 4:16)

12. If you were to develop an all-encompassing scriptural mission statement, in one sentence for your local body of believers, what would it say?

Practical Points to Consider

Unanswered or Additional Relevant Questions

Prayer

Heavenly Father, thank you for your love, mercy, and grace. Thank you for giving me life. Help me to always see you in our beautiful planet and appreciate the nurturing home you created for us. May I be mindful every day that you give me the breath of life, the ability to work and earn a living, the opportunity to engage in fellowship with others in the body of Christ, and a holy purpose for walking this planet until you call me to my eternal home. In Jesus's name I pray. Amen.

Journaling

Lesson 4
Being Chosen by God Is His Gift

But we ought always to thank God for you, brothers and sisters loved by the Lord, because God chose you as first fruits to be saved through the sanctifying work of the Spirit and through belief in the truth. He called you to this through our gospel, that you might share in the glory of our Lord Jesus Christ. (2 Thessalonians 2:13–14)

On the fourth day of Christmas my true love gave to me, being chosen, a righteous life to lead.

Observation

Twelve Gifts of Christmas, chapter 6, addresses God's gift of choosing us to have eternal life with him. This topic generates multiple questions in the minds of many people; questions that have been debated as long as humans have existed. Is there no god, one god, or many gods? If there is one Almighty God, who is he? Is there an eternity? If so, what will it look like? Is there a heaven and a hell? Do all paths lead to heaven? Everyone wants to know "the rest of the story." A brief review of the foundational beliefs of Buddhists, Hindus, Islamists, Jews, and Christians, to name a few; reveal significant basic differences regarding the answers to these questions. Christians believe in one Almighty God, Creator of everything, and eternal life with him through faith in his Son, Jesus Christ.

Robert N. McKaig, a nineteenth-century Indiana minister, in his book, *The Life and Times of the Holy Spirit*, speaks of finding God, writing:

> John Wesley says that no man living is without some . . . grace and every degree of grace is a degree of life. There is a measure of light that enlightens every man that comes into the world.. . . David Brainerd [(1718–1747), an American minister and missionary to Delaware Indians in New Jersey] found American Indians who believed in God who, when they could not dissuade their companions from drinking and carousing, would run away into the woods, crying unto the Good Spirit, though they had never heard the voice of a missionary.
>
> Bishop William Taylor [Methodist Episcopal missionary] found a great many heathens in Africa who believed in the God of the universe and worshiped him.. . . One poor woman in the depths of Africa, broke out in the most plaintive

cry when he preached Jesus unto her. "Oh, that is he who has come to me. So often in my prayers, but I couldn't find out who he was.

The theology that declares that all who have not heard of the birth at Bethlehem, or the death on Calvary, can have no benefit from the Atonement of Christ, is certainly contrary to the word of God, and is irresistibly and universally denied by the common judgment and conscience of man. For if some vagrant ship should carry you to a far off heathen island where no single ear had ever heard the first word about Christ, underneath the thick crust of savage life you will find the same old reaching after God that you left behind you in the streets and pews of home."[1]

God doesn't stop wooing us, once we give our lives to Jesus Christ as Lord and Savior. He continues to help us develop a deeper knowledge of who he is by revealing himself to us; sometimes in very intimate, unexpected ways. The author has stated:

"My wife, Susie, and I love vacations at the beach.. . . But there is one vacation I will never forget as long as I have my memory. In 2013, I had the opportunity to spend two weeks in a penthouse condo on the twentieth floor overlooking the Gulf of Mexico. The balcony off the living room faced due west with an amazing panoramic view. We checked into the condo on Saturday afternoon. That evening I was, as usual, sitting on the balcony near sunset watching the waves. There were no clouds on the horizon and we had an unobstructed view of a spectacular sunset. Our vacation had gotten off to a perfect start. But the best was yet to come.

The next day, on Sunday evening, shortly before sunset I had not yet gone onto the balcony. I heard a faint noise in the condo but couldn't identify the source. Finally, I realized the noise had to be coming from outside the building. I walked onto the balcony and saw a lone figure standing on the beach at the water's edge. No one was around him. The man was dressed in full Scottish regalia from head to toe; complete with Balmoral hat, kilt, and the knee-high socks with tasseled garters. I listened as he played Amazing Grace and America the Beautiful on his bagpipes as the sun slowly disappeared into the ocean.

The Lord had come to visit with me in a very special way. It was a brief, magnificent worship service unlike any I have experienced in a church building. I was moved in a profound way by such a gracious gift. I never saw or heard the Scotsman again. The Lord reminded me he is with me every day; in the church building, at work, or at the beach. The God of all creation came to me; met me where I was; just to spend time with me. He has always been willing to meet me where I am. I'm convinced just as God provided me with a "special time," he will also provide me with opportunities to spend "special time" with others on his behalf."[2]

Contemplation

(Suggested reading – Deuteronomy 4:29; Psalm 14:2; Acts 17:26-27)

1. Is it God's desire for all humans to seek and find him? Why or why not?

(Suggested reading – 1 Chronicles 28:9; Psalm 98:2; Isaiah 65:1-2; Jeremiah 24:7; Amos 4:13)

2. Why would a lost soul choose to seek God while living as an unrepentant sinner and his enemy?

(Suggested reading – Ecclesiastes 3:11 & 20; Ecclesiastes 12:1 & 5-7; Matthew 25:46)

3. What has God set in the human heart according to Ecclesiastes 3:11? How, if at all, does this relate to seeking God?

4. Is there evidence, outside of Scripture, that God designed us to seek him?

5. Have you ever observed something, concluding it was God who caused it and wanted you to know he did it? Give examples if you can.

6. How does it impact your faith knowing God wants you to seek and find him?

Inspiration

Hugh P. Hughes (1847–1902), was a Welsh Methodist clergyman and religious reformer. In his book, *Essential Christianity*, he writes about living in Christ:

> "Can you imagine any more imperfect or unworthy conception of Christianity than that Christ came to save us from hell? This statement is true, of course. But that was not his main object. His main object was that we might 'have life, and have it abundantly' (John 10:10). Neither to take us out of hell nor to take us into heaven but to give us his own life, to make us like himself did Christ die and rise again. That is the glorious purpose of his [resurrected] life. Have you this true life? Do you so share it as to be in conscious fellowship with Christ?
>
> At St. James's Hall . . . at the close of the service, a Canadian gentleman came into the vestry. I had been speaking of union with Christ. 'That is the very thing I want,' he said. 'I realize now, as never before, that although I have been a Christian, I have never been conscious of this union with

Christ. An aching void in my heart has been filled. I lacked something; now I have it.' This is our true life, this is the only real life, the life that comes to us as the 'free gift' of God.. . .

He [Christ] gives us a new life, his own life, that we may lead a Christ-like life. The whole ethical object of Christianity is summed up in the phrase 'Christ-like life.' You are a Christian if you do what Christ did.. . . Our duty is not merely to get to heaven, but to lead a Christ-like life on Earth."[3]

Response

(Suggested reading – Mark 2:17; John 6:44 & 64-65; 1 Corinthians 1:9 & 23-24)

7. What do Jesus's statements in John 6:44 and John 6:64-65 mean to you? Can we have faith in Jesus Christ as Lord and Savior without being "drawn by the Father?" Why or why not?

(Suggested reading – Matthew 28:19-20; Mark 16:15; Luke 24:46-48; Acts 2:42; 1 Corinthians 16:15-16)

8. Is there more to God's calling once a person has accepted his gift of grace through faith in his Son Jesus Christ? If so, what?

(Suggested reading – 1 Corinthians 11:1; Ephesians 4:1-3 & 5:1-2; 1 Peter 2:21-22; 1 John 2:5-6)

9. What do you believe is "the calling" referenced in Ephesians 4:1?

(Suggested reading – John 15:1-9; Colossians 1:9-11)

10. What are some of the ways in which we might "live worthy" of the calling?

(Suggested reading – Leviticus 11:44-45 & 20:26; Acts 13:2; 2 Corinthians 6:4 & 6; 2 Timothy 1:9; 2 Peter 1:3-4)

11. For those who do accept Jesus Christ as Lord and Savior, to what does God call them according to 2 Timothy 1:9? In this passage, what does "holy" mean to you?

(Suggested reading – Romans 8:28; 2 Corinthians 5:17-20; Ephesians 2:10)

12. For those who do accept Jesus Christ as Lord and Savior, to what does God call them according to Ephesians 2:10?

Practical Points to Consider

Unanswered or Additional Relevant Questions

Prayer

Heavenly Father, thank you for your love and mercy. Thank you for extending your gift of grace to me by drawing me to your Son Jesus. Help me to focus on eternal matters; always striving to live in Christ; seeking opportunities to bring glory to you, and benefit the kingdom of heaven. In Jesus's name I pray. Amen.

Journaling

Twelve Gifts of Christmas - From Our Heavenly Father - Study Guide

Lesson 5

Our Faith in God Comes From Him

For by the grace given me I say to every one of you: Do not think of yourself more highly than you ought, but rather think of yourself with sober judgment, in accordance with the faith God has distributed to each of you. (Romans 12:3)

On the fifth day of Christmas my true love gave to me, faith, so in him I could believe.

Observation

Twelve Gifts of Christmas, chapter 7, addresses God giving us the faith to believe. The author has discussed receiving swimming lessons as a youngster at the YMCA.

> "I'll never forget my first lesson. The instructor told us he couldn't teach us how to swim unless we would trust him enough to go into the deep water with him. Then, one by one, he wrapped his arm over the shoulder and across the chest of a student and swam, pulling the pupil from the shallow end of the pool to the deep end as the student floated on his back. This was a piece of cake for me. After all, I had already been going into deep water alone. But one of the boys couldn't do it. He was too afraid to let this stranger carry him into deep water, even after seeing the instructor do the same thing with all the other boys.
>
> The instructor told the boy to go get dressed and that maybe he could take the class later when he was ready to go into the deep end of the pool. The boy was embarrassed and angry. The instructor apologized saying, "If you don't trust me, I can't teach you to swim." I didn't give the matter a second thought that day, though I've never forgotten the incident. This was my first vivid memory of faith in action, or rather a lack of it. I was being taught a fundamental principle that had eternal ramifications, though I didn't recognize it at the time."[1]

Contemplation

(Suggested reading – 2 Corinthians 4:18; Hebrews 3:6 & 11:1)

1. How does Hebrews 11:1 define faith?

(Suggested reading – Mark 9:21-24; John 20:25; James 1:5-8)

2. Is your faith in all of God's promises certain; sure? Do you have varying degrees of faith, depending upon the specific promise? Why or why not?

(Suggested reading – Psalm 33:6 & 9, 148:5; Hebrews 11:3; 2 Peter 3:5)

3. After faith is defined, what is the first example of it given in Hebrews 11:3?

(Suggested reading – Romans 10:17 & 12:3; 2 Peter 1:1)

4. From where does faith in God the Father and his Son Jesus Christ come?

5. I have heard it asked, "How can I believe in a God I can't even see?" For those who do not believe in Jesus Christ as Lord and Savior, are there practical ways they exhibit faith in other unseen or uncontrollable matters in their lives?

(Suggested reading – Romans 3:22, 4:13 & 9:30; Philippians 3:9)

6. How, if at all, are faith and righteousness connected in the Bible?

Inspiration

The Bible is clear regarding the critical nature of faith in the life of a believer:

> And without faith it is impossible to please God, because anyone who comes to him must believe that he exists and that he rewards those who earnestly seek him (Hebrews 11:6).

James B. Walker (1805–1887), in his book, *The Doctrine of the Holy Spirit*, addresses faith saying:

> "Faith in the living example and dying love of Christ are both necessary. A living conscience and heart are the only true motives in the service of God. These are awakened by a sense of God in truth, and by Christ's suffering in the flesh for us. Good works for the temporal and spiritual good of man are the only true life; these are produced by conformity of the human will by love to the will of Christ.[2]

> Men can be purified only by obeying the truth through the Spirit.... If we 'abide in Christ' by faith, 'and his word abide in us' by understanding, we shall then have both the impulse of the Spirit and the guidance of the Word. Prayer will be answered; and we 'shall neither be barren nor unfruitful in the knowledge of our Lord and Savior Jesus Christ [2 Peter 1:8 KJV].'[3]

> In the life of every true Christian, conscience and love will rule; and the fruit of the Spirit, borne on all the branches united to Christ, will be 'love, joy, peace, long-suffering, gentleness, goodness, faith, meekness, and temperance.'[4]

In all things the Christian has faith in God. He believes God hears prayer. He sees the divine hand in all the providences that come to pass, small and great. He knows this is a state of probation, and that in a world of imperfection, where the good and the evil are mingled, the same external providence often befalls both classes. But he is sure nothing will befall him without some wise design, either to discipline him for some evil or to remove from him some temptation; and he relies with perfect assurance on the promise that 'all things work together for good to those who love God, to those who are the called according to his purpose [Romans 8:28].'"[5]

Response

7. Do you believe the example of faith given in Hebrews 11:3 is literal or figurative? Why or why not? Does it matter?

8. Of all the possible examples of faith available to God, why do you think he chose this particular one (Hebrews 11:3)?

(Suggested reading – Hebrews 11:7, 11-12, 17-19 & 31)

9. When you think about examples in Scripture of humans "stepping out in faith," or acting in a manner that reveals their faith, who comes to mind? Why? Have you known people during your life who also stepped out in faith?

(Suggested reading – Genesis 17:17 & 18:11-15; Exodus 3:10 & 4:10; Luke 1:13 & 18-20, 24:36-37)

10. Does the Bible speak of people who loved the Lord, yet struggled with doubt? Give examples if you can.

11. Do you have doubts or fears that impact your willingness to discuss topics such as miracles or spiritual warfare with others? Why or why not?

(Suggested reading – Genesis 3:1; Romans 14:23; 1 Corinthians 10:13; 2 Corinthians 10:5; James 4:7)

12. When you struggle with doubt, at times, how do you fight to overcome it?

Practical Points to Consider

Our Faith in God Comes From Him

Unanswered or Additional Relevant Questions

Prayer

Heavenly Father, thank you for your love, mercy, and grace. I thank you for extending the gift of faith to me while I was lost, willfully living in sin as your enemy. Help me to remain close to you, enveloped by your power and holiness; so that Satan's attacks against me, using my sinful nature and human doubt, won't be successful. In Jesus's name I pray. Amen.

Journaling

Our Faith in God Comes From Him

Lesson 6

The Desire to Live for God Is His Gift

With this in mind, we constantly pray for you, that our God may make you worthy of his calling, and that by his power he may bring to fruition your every desire for goodness and your every deed prompted by faith. (2 Thessalonians 1:11)

*On the sixth day of Christmas my true love gave to me,
a longing with his laws to agree.*

Observation

Twelve Gifts of Christmas, chapter 8, discusses God giving us the desire to live for him. In his book, *The Life and Times of the Holy Spirit*, Robert N. McKaig writes about the role of the Holy Spirit in developing agape [God's perfect] love within us.

> "The love of God is implanted in the heart when we are regenerated, but in that state, love is limited or feeble. It is not that deep, holy consuming love for sinners that Jesus had. Jesus sheds forth the Holy Spirit and that Spirit coming into us, sheds forth the love of God in our hearts. Then the love of God for the redemption of men will reach to the poorest, lowest, and farthest heathen.. . . . Our capacities will be filled with love.[1]
>
> Only when the heart is surcharged with divine love fresh from the heart of Jesus is it pained with such anguish for lost men that it can easily die, but cannot give them up."[2]

Contemplation

(Suggested reading – Genesis 6:5-6; Ecclesiastes 9:3; Jeremiah 17:9; Mark 7:21-23)

1. How does Scripture describe humans in their natural state?

(Suggested reading – Romans 7:18-23 & 8:5-8; Galatians 5:17; 1 Peter 2:11; 1 John 2:16)

2. What is the continual inner battle described in Scripture for those who desire to do good?

(Suggested reading – John 6:63; Romans 7:24-25 & 8:9-13; 1 John 2:17)

3. What solution does the Bible give for this life-long human battle?

(Suggested reading – Romans 6:6, 16-18 & 22; 1 Peter 2:16)

4. What does the Bible say about spiritual enslavement?

(Suggested reading – 1 Corinthians 12:6; Philippians 2:13; 2 Thessalonians 1:11 & 2:13-14)

5. How, then, does a lost soul, a self-absorbed slave to sin, develop a desire to live a godly life and serve others?

Preface to question 6 – According to Maslow's hierarchy of needs, in order of priority, the needs of humans are physiological (food, shelter and clothing); safety (personal security, employment); love and belonging (friendship, intimacy; and esteem); and self-actualization (becoming the best one can be).

6. Do you agree with Maslow's theory? Why or why not?

Inspiration

In his book, *The Life and Times of the Holy Spirit*, Robert N. McKaig writes about a real-life story of a soul sacrificing for Christ:

> "Did you ever hear the story of the Baptist Zulu Mission in Africa? Sir Henry Morton Stanley speaks of it as the greatest mission in the world. The founder, Mr. Henry Richards, was there seven years without a convert. One Sunday, he told them that something was wrong. Either he was not a missionary, or he was not preaching the gospel, or else the gospel was not the power of God unto the salvation of the Zulus. He said, 'I will tell you next Sunday what is the matter.'
>
> He and his wife read the Bible, prayed, fasted, and the next Sunday the house was full to hear his conclusion. After the service he said: 'I am sent as a missionary. The gospel is the power of God unto salvation, but I have not been preaching the gospel, but the law and morality. I will now try to preach the gospel and am going to live it.' So, he began at Matthew to tell the good news about Jesus. When he came to the Sermon on the Mount he read this sentence, 'Give to the one who asks you, and do not turn away from the one who wants to borrow from you.' He gave it the usual definition, but they shook their heads for they were all beggars. 'Come back next Sunday and I will tell you exactly what it means.'
>
> The next Sunday, he said it meant what it said. If they wanted anything he had and would ask him he would give it to them. If they wanted to borrow, he would lend them anything he had. After the benediction they went to his home and took everything that he had except one lounge. The

next morning two Zulus met on the corner and one said, 'Let us go to the home of the missionary and get something.' They went to his house and he gave them the lounge. When they were carrying out the lounge, one of them was so convicted by the Spirit that he began to cry. They knelt down, prayed, and he was converted. In two years 7,000 more were led to Christ."[3]

Response

(Suggested reading – Galatians 2:2 & 6; Philippians 2:3-11 & 3:7-11)

7. Do you think Christians should desire to be esteemed? Why or why not? If so, by whom?

_____

_____

_____

_____

_____

_____

Preface to question 8 – Some of the previous passages of Scripture in this lesson are less than flattering to humans. However, these were not discussed to heap guilt or shame on believers who struggle to live a Christ-like life every day.

(Suggested reading – Deuteronomy 8:12-14; Luke 7:41, 43 & 47; 2 Corinthians 13:5-6; Colossians 1:13-14; James 1:23-25)

8. What, then, are the practical, positive benefits of looking into the mirror of God's Word and assessing the "less than desirable" traits that exist in our natural state?

Preface to question 9 – Paul, in three of his letters listed below, gives us glimpses of how he viewed his inner self. These three views are arranged in order from his earlier to later writings.

(Suggested reading – 1 Corinthians 15:9; Ephesians 3:8; 1 Timothy 1:15)

9. How does Paul view himself? What changes do you see in his self-assessment? What do you believe caused these changes?

The Desire to Live for God Is His Gift

10. What changes, if any, do you see in the life of Apostle John over time? What do you believe caused these changes?

11. Are there others, either in Scripture or people you know personally, whose humility and love have increased as their time walking with the Lord increased?

12. What changes have you seen in your life as you have progressed from an unsaved soul, to a young Christian, to where you are in your walk with Jesus Christ today?

Practical Points to Consider

The Desire to Live for God Is His Gift

Unanswered or Additional Relevant Questions

Prayer

Heavenly Father, thank you for your love, mercy, and grace. Thank you for building within me the desire to live for you. Help me to be ever-vigilant as Satan seeks to eliminate, or at least diminish, my desire to serve you. Protect and enable me by the power of your Holy Spirit. In Jesus's name I pray. Amen.

Journaling

The Desire to Live for God Is His Gift

Lesson 7

The Holy Spirit – God's Power in Us

Peter replied, "Repent and be baptized, every one of you, in the name of Jesus Christ for the forgiveness of your sins. And you will receive the gift of the Holy Spirit." (Acts 2:38)

On the seventh day of Christmas my true love gave to me, his Spirit, my indwelling guarantee.

Observation

Twelve Gifts of Christmas, chapter 9, addresses the power of God's Holy Spirit residing within us. Alexander Patterson, in his book *The Greater Life and Work of Christ*, discusses the unparalleled power of the Holy Spirit.

> "We may look in reverent imagination upon the scene within the sepulcher [tomb or vault]. It is a low-roofed place, in which it is scarcely possible to stand erect. There lies the form we saw hanging on the cross. Loving hands have wrapped it in a clean linen cloth and fragrant spices. Limbs and head are carefully adjusted. No human body could be more truly dead than that one.. . .
>
> His heart was pierced by the soldier's spear, which probably emptied the entire blood from the body.. . . The tomb is closed by a stone which required the strength of several men to move. It was sealed and a guard of soldiers watched before it. No one of his own power had ever come out from the dead, and there was no prophet to work such a miracle. To human eyes all was hopeless. Except his own word and the predictions of Scripture, there was not a single ray of hope that Jesus would rise.. . . The Holy Spirit had never left that precious form. He is the giver of life. Now he simply exercises his office work. Therefore, life flows through that lifeless body.. . .
>
> A change, too, takes place in the body itself. It is the resurrection change. It becomes superior to natural laws; yet it was a real body. Jesus was afterward handled and felt, did eat and drink, was heard, spoken to, and recognized. It was true corporeal [flesh and blood] life but sustained by the

immediate power of the Holy Spirit. All the functions of the body were in a full state of perfection. It was the same yet not the same."[1]

George B. Thompson (1862–1930) ministered in West Virginia and New York. He also served as a missionary in Africa for four years. In his book, *The Ministry of the Spirit*, he describes the indwelling Holy Spirit from another aspect; presenting him in a very intimate way.

"The indwelling presence of the Spirit 'is the shepherd's mark upon the flock of the Lord Jesus, distinguishing them from the rest of the world. It is the goldsmith's stamp on the genuine sons of God, separating them from the dross [metal waste or impurity] and mass of false professors.' It is the king's own seal on those who are his peculiar people, proving them to be his own property. It is the pledge which the Redeemer gives to his believing disciples, while they are in the body, of the full redemption yet to come in the resurrection when the dead in Christ shall live again."[2]

Contemplation

1. By what names (not characteristics or attributes) is the Holy Spirit known in Scripture?

2. How would you describe the fundamental characteristics or attributes of the Spirit of God using one word or short phrases?

3. Suppose someone unfamiliar with the Bible has just asked you to explain to them in simple terms, "Who or what is the Holy Spirit and why do Christians need him?" How might you respond?

(Suggested reading – Acts 5:30-32; Ephesians 1:13-14; 1 John 3:23-24)

4. Scripture, on numerous occasions, speaks of the Holy Spirit dwelling in Christians. Why, if at all, is this important to the believer?

(Suggested reading – Romans 12:6-8; 1 Corinthians 12:8-10)

5. What are the spiritual gifts listed in 1 Corinthians 12:8-10 and Romans 12:7-8? Are there other spiritual gifts?

(Suggested reading – 1 Corinthians 1:5-7 & 12:31)

6. Do you believe each Christian has none, some, or all of these gifts? Why or why not?

Inspiration

According to a US Geological Survey fact sheet by Steve Brantley and Bobbie Myers regarding the Mount St. Helens eruption:

> "The first sign of activity at Mount St. Helens in the spring of 1980 was a series of small earthquakes that began on March 16.. . . On May 18 . . . the volcano's bulge and summit slid away in a huge landslide—the largest on Earth in recorded history.. . .
>
> The blast cloud traveled as far as 17 miles northward from the volcano and the landslide traveled about 14 miles west.. . . Swift avalanches of hot ash, pumice, and gas (pyroclastic flows) poured out of the crater at 50 to 80 miles per hour and spread as far as 5 miles to the north.. . . Prevailing winds blew 520 million tons of ash eastward across the US and caused complete darkness in Spokane, Washington, 250 miles from the volcano.. . ."

- More than thirteen hundred feet of mountain was removed from the top and side of Mount St. Helens.
- The landslide of these 3.7 billion cubic yards of earth, traveling between 70 and 150 miles per hour, covered 23 square miles.
- The lateral blast, traveling at 300 miles per hour, deposited 250 million cubic yards of debris over 230 square miles.
- Four billion board feet of timber, enough to build about 300,000 two-bedroom homes, were blown down.
- The volcano plume reached about 80,000 feet in less than 15 minutes.

- 1.4 billion cubic yards of ash spread across the US in 3 days and circled Earth in 15 days.
- Twenty-four megatons of thermal energy were released.[3]

According to the National Museum of the US Air Force, the atomic bomb "Fat Man," which was dropped on Nagasaki during World War II, released an explosive force of about 20,000 tons of dynamite.[4] The thermal energy released by the Mount St. Helens' blast was, by my calculation, approximately 1,200 times more powerful than the "Fat Man" atomic bomb.

In his book, *The Ministry of the Spirit*, George B. Thompson discusses a very different kind of power; that of the Holy Spirit working in the Christian life.

> "Spiritual or evangelical power is designated by the word dunamis, as in Luke 24:49.. . . It is this word dunamis from which dynamite, dynamos, dynamics, dynasty, etc., are derived. If we endeavor to analyze the elements of this power in itself, I think we shall fail. It is spiritual and invisible. All we can do is to trace the circumstances under which this power is given, and the results which flow from it. Indeed, power is in its nature indescribable. It is known simply by its results. Gravitation, that greatest of all material powers, ceaselessly active, everywhere potent, is wholly beyond our research, or even our conception.[5]

> Christianity is a power. It is God's almighty power. It is the same power that made the worlds, and swings them in space.[6]

> The Spirit was to be given as a regenerating agent. Without this the sacrifice of Christ would have been of no avail.. . . Sin could be resisted and overcome only through the mighty agency of the third person of the Godhead, who would

come with no modified energy, but in the fullness of divine power. It is the Spirit that makes effectual what has been wrought out by the world's Redeemer.. . . In the Christian life Jesus Christ is its rule, the Holy Spirit its power."[7]

Response

7. What is the greatest display of power you have ever witnessed? What was your reaction to this display? How does that compare to the power residing inside a believer?

8. How has God displayed his power through humans in the past?

(Suggested reading – Romans 14:1-2; 1 Corinthians 8:9-13)

9. Does the Holy Spirit give spiritual gifts in varying degrees to different persons? What are the strongest spiritual gifts the Holy Spirit has given to you?

(Suggested reading – 1 Corinthians 3:16-17; 2 Corinthians 1:21-22; Ephesians 3:6)

10. What are some of the eternal benefits of the Holy Spirit dwelling in Christians?

(Suggested reading – John 15:5; 1 Corinthians 2:4-5 & 6:19-20; 2 Corinthians 4:6-7; Ephesians 1:17)

11. What are some of the earthly benefits or considerations of the Holy Spirit dwelling in Christians?

12. How can a believer know, as a practical matter, that the Holy Spirit is actively working in their life?

Practical Points to Consider

Unanswered or Additional Relevant Questions

Prayer

Heavenly Father, thank you for your love, mercy, and grace. Thank you for giving me your indwelling Holy Spirit who will guide me to live the life to which you have called me. Help me to have the wisdom and courage to follow the leading of your Spirit. May my life benefit your kingdom and bring glory to you. It is in the name of Jesus Christ, your Son and my Lord, that I pray. Amen.

Journaling

Twelve Gifts of Christmas - From Our Heavenly Father - Study Guide

Lesson 8

The Fruit of the Holy Spirit – God Producing in Us

But the fruit of the Spirit is love, joy, peace, patience, kindness, goodness, faithfulness, gentleness, and self-control. (Galatians 5:22–23 ESV)

On the eighth day of Christmas my true love gave to me,
his holy fruit of which I am a trustee.

Observation

Twelve Gifts of Christmas, chapter 10, addresses how God uses the fruit of the Holy Spirit to produce benefits for the kingdom of heaven through us. George B. Thompson, in his book, *The Ministry of the Spirit,* discusses the inability of humanity to save itself and the power of the One who is mighty to save.

> "Man by nature is 'without strength,' Satan's captive, a slave to sin. He is able to conquer the sea.. . . . He navigates the boundless expanse in safety. He turns his attention to the heavens, searches out the mysteries of the stars, and traces their orbits with precision.. . . By intellectual force and marvelous inventions, he subdues the face of the world and compels the forces of nature to be his servants. He makes laws by which nations are able to govern millions of subjects. He institutes war, which destroys empires, blots out dynasties, and changes the map of the world.
>
> In short, he executes all that is included in history, and the marvelous achievements about us, showing his tremendous energy in almost everything that stirs the silence, changing the conditions of the world. But, though able to subdue kingdoms and conquer the forces of nature, he cannot conquer himself. He cannot of himself restrain his own passions and impulses. He stands humbled and vanquished by sin, its slave and lawful captive.. . .
>
> Man has the power to overstep the moral boundary of his being, and deviate from that which is right. He has within him a power, the law of sin and death, which is continu-

ally urging him to do so. But there is help for him. There is One who is mighty to save, who, through the power of the Spirit, is able to cope with sin, change the carnal heart, transform the life, and make those who have been the slaves of sin more than conquerors. The believer in Christ has been quickened, resurrected from the dead, and knows the exceeding greatness of his power. He understands from experience what it is to conquer temptation and live the victorious life of faith; triumphing through the Spirit over the powers of darkness."[1]

Contemplation

1. The fruit of the Holy Spirit, in Galatians 5:22-23, is described as singular, rather than plural. Is this significant to you? Why or why not?

(Suggested reading – John 3:16; 1 Corinthians 13:13; Colossians 3:14; 1 John 4:8 & 16)

2. What is the first part or aspect of the fruit of the Holy Spirit listed? What significance, if any, do you attach to this?

3. What is the most difficult part, for you, of expressing love to all others? Why?

(Suggested reading – Acts 16:34; Romans 14:17 & 15:13; 1 Peter 1:8-9)

4. What is a biblical definition of joy and from where does it come? How does it differ from the worldly definition of joy?

(Suggested reading – Romans 5:1 & 8:6; Ephesians 2:14; Colossians 3:15)

5. What is a biblical definition of peace and from where does it come? How does that differ from the worldly definition of peace?

(Suggested reading – Ephesians 4:2; 1 Timothy 1:16; James 5:10)

6. What role does patience play in our relationship with others? What distinction, if any, do you make between patience and perseverance?

___

Inspiration

In his book, *The Life and Times of the Holy Spirit*, Robert N. McKaig discusses the beauty of the fruit of the Spirit.

> "These are the nine clusters of the fruit of the Spirit. What beautiful clusters they are that the Spirit intends to bring forth in every one of our lives!
>
> Perfect love to God and man!
> Joy inexpressible and full of glory!
> Peace that passes all understanding!
> Long suffering with joyfulness!
> Gentleness without softness!
> Goodness without insipidity [dullness]!
> Faithfulness without stubbornness!
> Meekness without murmurings!
> Self-control in abstaining from every form of evil, never lifted up with increase, or cast down with loss!

What beautiful clusters! Let us endeavor to bear them all by receiving and abiding in the Holy Spirit."[2]

But how do these beautiful clusters present themselves in the life of a believer? George B. Thompson, in his book, *The Ministry of the Spirit*, discusses one of the changes the Holy Spirit brings to the heart of a Christian.

> "When the Spirit is allowed to abide in our hearts, it will lead us to give our lives for those who are lost. It lays upon every heart a clear burden for this work. The great apostle said he had 'great heaviness and continual sorrow' [Romans 9:2-3] in his heart for his people rejecting Christ. Likewise, in every heart that yields to the Spirit's gentle influence there will be a burden for lost souls.. . . The Lord gives us the baptism of the Spirit for service. . .
>
> One day from the deck of an ocean liner a boat was seen drifting in mid-ocean. It had come from a sinking vessel. A boat and crew were sent in pursuit. In the bottom of the drifting boat a man was found, exhausted and unconscious. As he was lifted up and taken into the other boat, he partially revived. The first feeble words heard from his lips were, 'There's another man in the boat.' Then he again became unconscious.
>
> Saved himself, his first thought was to have another saved. This incident illustrates the spirit of the true Christian. One of the first evidences of the indwelling of the Holy Spirit is an interest in some other soul, in the other man in the boat, in the man who is the farthest down. The Scriptures abound in examples of personal work for souls by those who were Spirit filled."[3]

Response

7. Why do you believe kindness and goodness are listed as components in the fruit of the Spirit? Aren't these expected of everyone?

_____

_____

_____

_____

_____

_____

_____

(Suggested reading – Isaiah 40:11; Matthew 11:29-30; John 10:11; Titus 3:2)

8. What role does gentleness play in our relationship with others?

_____

_____

_____

_____

_____

_____

_____

The Fruit of the Holy Spirit - God Producing in Us

9. What part or aspect of the fruit of the Spirit do you believe is most closely related to forgiveness? Why?

(Suggested reading – Proverbs 16:32; Titus 2:11-12; James 3:7-10; 2 Peter 1:5-8)

10. In what way, if any, is self-control markedly different from the other parts or aspects of the fruit of the Spirit?

11. From a biblical perspective, can I truthfully say, "That's not my gift" when referring to one or more parts of the fruit of the Spirit?

12. Which part or aspect of the fruit of the Holy Spirit shows in your life most consistently?

Practical Points to Consider

Unanswered or Additional Relevant Questions

Prayer

Heavenly Father, thank you for your love, mercy, and grace. Thank you for placing your Holy Spirit within me; providing me with everything I need to accomplish your will here on Earth. Help me to utilize those parts of your Spirit that are the strongest within me and develop those parts that are weaker, so I might become more effective in bringing glory to you. In Jesus's name I pray. Amen.

Journaling

The Fruit of the Holy Spirit – God Producing in Us

Lesson 9

The Word of God – His Gift of Revelation

For the word of God is alive and active. Sharper than any double-edged sword, it penetrates even to dividing soul and spirit, joints and marrow; it judges the thoughts and attitudes of the heart. (Hebrews 4:12)

On the ninth day of Christmas my true love gave to me, the flawless truth, his loving decree.

Observation

Twelve Gifts of Christmas, chapter 11, addresses the gift of God's Word given to us. Laurence W. Scott, a nineteenth-century minister in Texas, discusses those who do not believe in Jesus as the Son of God or the Bible as God's Word. In his book, *The Great Crisis in the Life of Christ*, he writes:

> "Suffice it to say that the writers of epistles in the New Testament, the apostolic and Christian fathers, and all the witnesses friendly to Jesus, attest the historic value of those books. Their testimony is confirmed by his bitterest enemies, like Porphyry, Celsus, Julian; and by standard historians like Josephus and Tacitus.[1]
>
> Every material fact of gospel history, except the resurrection of Jesus, is either corroborated by an unbelieving historian, or admitted by an ancient or modern disbeliever.[2]
>
> But when we remember that their [early writings about Christian events] general truthfulness was never questioned by any of the early enemies of the cross, the case is still stronger. Celsus, Porphyry and Julian never denied that these books are historical.. . . . If those early and inveterate [having a long-established habit and unlikely to change] enemies of the religion of Jesus could have denied the authenticity of these books they would have done so. But they made no attempt in that direction. If the books were untrue, then was the time to show it. No research can do it now, for every discovery in Christian antiquities but strengthens the argument in their favor.[3]

The celebrated French infidel [a person who does not believe in religion], Ernest Renan, said: 'I have traveled through the evangelical province in every direction; I have visited Jerusalem, Hebron, and Samaria. Scarcely any locality important in the history of Jesus has escaped me. All this history which, at a distance, seems floating in the clouds of an unreal world, thus assumed a body, a solidity which astonished me. The striking accord of the texts and the places, the wonderful harmony of the evangelical ideal, with the landscape which served as its setting, were to me as a revelation.. . . Thenceforth through the narratives of Matthew and Mark, instead of an abstract being, which one would say had never existed, I saw a wonderful human form live and move.'[4]

Prof. Frederick G. Wright has stated, 'Close examination of the documents themselves [Matthew, Mark, and Luke] amply confirms their early date, showing that their writers were contemporaneous with the facts narrated. The destruction of Jerusalem in the year AD 70 was a turning point in the world's history. The changes that took place in Palestine in the whole social, political, and religious conditions were sweeping.'

The Temple and its service disappeared. The Jews were scattered to the four corners of the Earth. The Roman power came into absolute sway. But the first three Gospels betray no knowledge of these changes. Their language, their references to geography, to social, political, and religious conditions are wholly such as would be used by writers in the second quarter of the first century."[5]

Contemplation

(Suggested reading – Genesis 3:8-13 & 15:1; Exodus 7:17-18; Judges 4:6)

1. Before Jesus Christ came to Earth as a man, how did God communicate with humans?

\
\
\
\
\
\
\

(Suggested reading – John 13:12-15; Romans 1:17 & 10:17; 1 Corinthians 2:10; Ephesians 6:18)

2. How has God communicated with humans since Jesus Christ ascended into heaven?

\
\
\
\
\
\

(Suggested reading – Psalm 119:89; John 1:1 & 14; 2 Timothy 3:16)

3. How does Scripture describe itself in supernatural ways?

_____

_____

_____

_____

_____

_____

_____

(Suggested reading – Psalm 119:9 & 11; John 17:17; 1 Corinthians 15:2)

4. How does Scripture refer to itself regarding assisting Christians while living on Earth?

_____

_____

_____

_____

_____

_____

(Suggested reading – Romans 8:26-27 & 12:2; Hebrews 4:12)

5. What does Scripture mean by calling itself alive, active, dividing soul and spirit, judging the thoughts and attitudes of the heart (Hebrews 4:12)?

(Suggested reading – Romans 1:16; 2 Corinthians 10:3-4; Ephesians 6:12 & 17)

6. In the description of the full armor of God, why is the word of God described as the sword of the Spirit (Ephesians 6:17)?

Inspiration

Henry M. Morris (1918–2006) received his PhD in hydraulic engineering. He served as a professor and department chairman for civil engineering at Virginia Tech. He was also a founder of the Institute for Creation Research, serving as president and then president emeritus. Morris was a staunch defender of the historical accuracy of the Bible and the critical nature of the reliability of God's Word in the lives of believers. In his book, *The Genesis Record*, he wrote:

> "If the Bible were somehow expurgated [had objectionable matter removed] of the Book of Genesis (as many people today would prefer), the rest of the Bible would be incomprehensible. It would be like a building without a ground floor, or a bridge with no support. The books of the Old Testament, narrating God's dealings with the people of Israel, would be provincial and bigoted, were they not set in the context of God's developing purposes for all mankind, as laid down in the early chapters of Genesis.[6]

> There are at least 165 passages in Genesis that are either directly quoted or clearly referred to in the New Testament.... There exist over one hundred quotations or direct references to Genesis 1—11 in the New Testament.... On at least six different occasions, Jesus Christ himself quoted from or referred to something or someone in one of these chapters, including specific reference to each of the first seven chapters.... Furthermore, in not one of these many instances where the Old or New Testament refers to Genesis is there the slightest evidence that the writers regarded the events or personages as mere myths or allegories. To the contrary, they viewed Genesis as absolutely historical, true, and authoritative.[7]

It is quite impossible, therefore, for one to reject the historicity and divine authority of the book of Genesis without undermining, and in effect, repudiating [refusing to accept or be associated with], the authority of the entire Bible."[8]

Response

(Suggested reading – 1 Samuel 3:1; 2 Chronicles 15:2-3; Psalm 74:9; Amos 8:11-12)

7. Before Jesus Christ came to Earth as a man, was there ever a scarcity of God's Word available to humans?

8. Is there a scarcity of God's Word in the world today?

(Suggested reading – Galatians 1:8-9; 2 Timothy 4:3; Revelation 12:13 & 17)

9. Who or what are the main opponents of, or detractors from, God's Word today?

(Suggested reading – 1 Chronicles 21:1 & 7; Matthew 4:1-3 & 13:18-19)

10. How does Satan oppose or detract from the Word of God?

11. Why is it so important for Satan to discredit God's Word?

12. Is the Holy Bible you hold in your hand today the perfectly true, flawless word of God as he intended it to be? Why or why not?

Practical Points to Consider

Unanswered or Additional Relevant Questions

Prayer

Heavenly Father, thank you for your love, mercy, and grace. Thank you for the precious gift of your Word. May I appreciate, daily, the Bibles that are in my home. They are greatly desired by many around the world who have none. Only by knowing your truth can I identify the deception of those who oppose you. Help me to understand what your Word says, to be convinced it is the flawless, eternal truth; and follow its guidance in my daily life. In Jesus's name I pray. Amen.

Journaling

The Word of God - His Gift of Revelation

Lesson 10

Adopted by God – His Gift to Spiritual Orphans

Yet to all who did receive him, to those who believed in his name, he gave the right to become children of God. (John 1:12)

On the tenth day of Christmas my true love gave to me, a place of mine within his family.

Observation

Twelve Gifts of Christmas, chapter 12, addresses God's gift of adopting us into his eternal family. The godly model of relationship we see throughout Scripture is one of a family. For many of us, our most intimate, loving relationships have been developed within this unit; parents, siblings, spouses, and children. For just a moment, think about a cherished friend or family member; someone in whose presence you found love, acceptance, and belonging. We all have a deep-seated need to be loved, wanted, valued. Because of that, we also have a strong desire to avoid abandonment, ridicule, and rejection. These loving, intimate relationships provide us with a sense of safety; being accepted for who we are. Our Creator wants to be our Father. His desire is for us to love him as he loves us.

George C. Lorimer, in his book, *The Galilean*, paints a loving picture of Almighty God.

> "Though humanity through sin denies its sonship, though it may repudiate [refuse to accept or be associated with] the divine parent, and like the prodigal have wandered into a far country, and though it needs the renewal of the Holy Ghost [Spirit] to impart the consciousness of adoption, God is still the Father seeking to save the lost, wayward child. Oh, my brethren, there is something to inspire worship in such a sublime conception, a being who is all-pervasive Spirit, who fills immensity with himself, and who is also Father, loving with a Father's heart the meanest of his creatures. Who can hear this and not worship?"[1]

Contemplation

(Suggested reading – Matthew 7:11 & 16:17; Galatians 4:6)

1. In the Gospel According to Matthew (NIV), Jesus refers to the heavenly "Father" no less than 35 times. In these passages, God is the "Father" of whom? What type of relationship does this name imply?

(Suggested reading – Genesis 9:6; Psalm 119:73; 1 Corinthians 11:7)

2. I have heard it said, referring to all of humanity, "We are all God's children." Is this correct according to the Bible?

(Suggested reading – John 1:9-13; 3:3-8 & 8:39-44; Galatians 3:26-27)

3. Who are the children of God according to Scripture?

(Suggested reading – Romans 8:14-16 & 23; Galatians 4:4-5)

4. What does the Bible say about the adoption of humans into the family of God?

(Suggested reading – Matthew 25:34; Romans 8:17-19; Galatians 4:7; Revelation 21:6-7)

5. What does Scripture say about the children of God being heirs and having an inheritance?

(Suggested reading – 2 Corinthians 4:4; Ephesians 2:1-2; 1 John 5:19)

6. Who is in control of Earth at the present time?

Inspiration

American Tract Society discusses the Yoruba, a native group in Africa, in their book, *The Gift of the Knees*, writing:

> These converted idolators have a peculiarly expressive term to describe prayer. They call it the gift of the knees.[2]

> There is a tendency to separate too widely the life of the soul and the life of the body. Religion and prayer have been too often considered matters adapted only to certain times, as if the Christian man were to draw his "vital breath" at stated intervals of time, to live his true Christian life on one day of the seven only, or at least not on every day and hour of the week.... Christians need to cultivate more thoroughly the gift of the knees.[3]

In his book, *Life of St. Francis Of Assisi*, Paul Sabatier discusses the role of access to the Father in the lives of believers:

> "For him [St. Francis], as for St. Paul and St. Augustine, conversion was a radical, complete change; the act of will by which man wrests himself from the slavery of sin and places himself under the yoke of divine authority. Thenceforth, prayer becomes a necessary act of life; ceases to be a magic formula. It is an impulse of the heart. It is reflection and meditation rising above the common places of this mortal life, to enter into the mystery of the divine will and conform itself to it. It is the act of the atom which understands its littleness, but which desires, though only by a single note, to be in harmony with the divine symphony...

When we reach these heights we belong not to a sect, but to humanity. We are like those wonders of nature which the accident of circumstances has placed upon the territory of this or that people, but which belong to all the world. In fact, they belong to no one, or rather they are the common and inalienable property of the entire human race. Homer, Shakespeare, Dante, Goethe, Michelangelo, and Rembrandt belong to us all as much as the ruins of Athens or Rome, or, rather, they belong to those who love them most and understand them best."[4]

Response

(Suggested reading – Exodus 20:18-19; Matthew 27:50-51; Hebrews 6:19-20, 9:7-8 & 10:19-22)

7. Was access to God the Father different before Jesus came to Earth as a man and after he ascended into heaven? If so, how?

(Suggested reading – Isaiah 59:2; Matthew 7:7-8; John 15:7; 1 Thessalonians 5:17-18; James 4:3; 1 John 5:14-15)

8. Through faith in Jesus Christ, we are now given direct access to God anytime, anywhere. What are some foundational principles regarding our communications with our heavenly Father?

Preface to question 9 – According to the US Department of Health and Human Services: since fiscal year 2012, the number of children in foster care on the last day of each fiscal year through 2017 increased from 392,000 in 2012 to 437,000 in 2017. The number of children waiting for adoption also grew from a low of 102,000 in 2013 to 125,000 in 2018.[5]

9. Why do you believe there are so many children waiting for adoption in America, one of the richest nations on Earth?

10. How, if at all, is our spiritual adoption into the family of God similar to earthly adoptions in America?

(Suggested reading – 2 Corinthians 13:11; Galatians 6:2, 9-10)

11. What are some of the earthly benefits of being part of the family of God?

12. Understanding, at least partially, the price God paid through his Son to adopt you into his family; how does that impact your daily walk with Jesus Christ?

Practical Points to Consider

Unanswered or Additional Relevant Questions

Prayer

Heavenly Father, thank you for your love, mercy, and grace. Thank you for the sacrifice of your Son, Jesus, so I might have the hope of eternal life with you. Lord, I don't understand so great a love; but I believe in it and accept it. Help me, daily, to live a life that will bring glory to you and your kingdom. In Jesus's name I pray. Amen.

Journaling

Lesson 11

A Living Hope – God's Gift of Encouragement

Praise be to the God and Father of our Lord Jesus Christ! In his great mercy he has given us new birth into a living hope through the resurrection of Jesus Christ from the dead, and into an inheritance that can never perish, spoil or fade. This inheritance is kept in heaven for you. (1 Peter 1:3–4)

On the eleventh day of Christmas my true love gave to me, a living hope, one day his face to see.

Observation

Twelve Gifts of Christmas, chapter 13, addresses the living hope God gives to those who believe in Jesus Christ as Lord and Savior. Alexander Pope (c. 1688–1744), was an English poet. In his book, *An Essay on Man*, he wrote: "Hope springs eternal in the human breast."[1]

But is this statement true of humanity, generally speaking? The author has written:

> "I've never met a single person who said, 'I don't want to have hope. I'd rather live without it.' We don't have to be Rhodes scholars to understand such a concept is preposterous on its face. We all have desires which we sincerely hope will be realized; a happy marriage, a healthy family, friends who truly love us. Life would be so dark and dreary without it; because despair is the opposite of hope.
>
> I am convinced despair, like an invisible virulent flu, is a spiritual disease spreading through America; infecting more of our population each day. There is an axiom [a statement or proposition accepted to be self-evidently true] found in various forms on the Internet regarding Christians. It goes something like this: 'We do not have a hopeless end, but an endless hope.' Our endless hope is also a present, living hope through the resurrection of Jesus Christ.
>
> Therefore, our message to the world is 'hope through the truth.' Why do I say that? Because our hope is in God's word which is the eternal, flawless truth. Our God, who is all-powerful and unchanging, has promised us eternal life if we have faith in the crucified, resurrected Jesus Christ as our Lord and Savior. Rest assured, God will deliver on his certain promise, in his own good time.

Conversely, worldly hope, many times, is nothing more than a wish which is unlikely to be realized; such as winning the lottery this month. Is it possible? Yes. But what are the odds? Astronomical. Such wishes have virtually no chance of occurring. To be sure, there are worldly hopes which have a reasonable, or even probable, chance of coming true. Still, such hopes are temporary at best; going to the grave with us. For the lost soul who understands there is an eternity, they hope everyone goes to heaven. Those who presume there is no eternity, heaven, or hell; have hope only for this life. Those who are without faith in Jesus Christ have no eternal hope."[2]

Contemplation

(Suggested reading – Titus 1:2-3 & 3:7; 1 Peter 1:3-4 & 3:21-22)

1. Why is the hope mentioned in 1 Peter 1:3 described as living? What is it and how do humans obtain it?

(Suggested reading – Job 8:11-13; Ephesians 2:12; 1 Thessalonians 4:13)

2. What hope does the world offer humanity?

(Suggested reading – Psalm 25:5; Matthew 12:18-21 & 19:29; Acts 23:6; Romans 15:13)

3. In whom or what does the Christian's hope lie?

(Suggested reading – Proverbs 11:7; 1 Corinthians 15:19 & 32)

4. What is the fate of those who place their hope in anyone or anything other than God's plan of salvation through the sacrifice and resurrection of Jesus Christ?

(Suggested reading – Psalm 42:11; Ecclesiastes 9:4; Lamentations 3:21-23)

5. How long does hope exist for those who are lost; without Jesus Christ?

(Suggested reading – Colossians 1:5; 2 Timothy 4:8; 1 Peter 1:4-5)

6. Where is the hope of Christians stored according to Colossians 1:5? What does this tell you about the ability of anyone who would desire to remove or destroy that hope?

_____

_____

_____

_____

Inspiration

I believe living hope is a rare, precious commodity on Earth. Without it there can be neither peace nor joy. How sad it is for a Christian who fails to realize or forgets their living hope in Christ. How glorious it is when a believer, who has temporarily forgotten, rediscovers the living hope that filled their soul when they first gave their life to Jesus.

Hardin E. Taliaferro (c. 1811–1875), formerly known as Mark H. Taliaferro, was a minister and junior editor of the South Western Baptist, a weekly newspaper in Tuskegee, Alabama. In his book, *The Grace of God Magnified*, the author speaks of a personal internal torment; a Christian who struggled with doubt for many years. Realizing his unworthiness in his sinful nature, he was unsure if Jesus truly loved him. He describes the precious work of grace through the Holy Spirit that ultimately produced lasting hope in his soul. This was accomplished when the Lord revealed to him that those who believe in the Christ as Lord and Savior are saved by the righteousness of Jesus, not human worthiness. Taliaferro writes:

- The more I examined my heart in the light of the holy law of God, the plainer my innate depravity appeared. The more I examined the character of God as revealed in his word, the plainer my unfitness to appear before him in a perfect righteousness was manifested. The disparity was overwhelming to my soul. I had such clear views of the holiness and justice of God and such deep views of the depravity of my heart and the sinfulness of my nature.[3]

- Christ's sufferings were clear to my mind. I saw that they were perfectly satisfactory to every claim which the moral government of God held against me.. . . By faith I beheld Christ Jesus; who, of God, was made unto me wisdom, righteousness, sanctification, and redemption. Condemnation and guilt left me instantaneously. I felt the power, and understood clearly the Bible doctrine of justification by faith, "without the deeds of the law." The doctrine of works and self-righteousness, as a ground of acceptance with God, was forever banished from my mind. My soul trusted on Christ, without fear, for salvation, and I was happy! .. . .

- The Father I devoutly praised for devising the scheme of salvation, by which I was justified; the Son for executing it; and the Holy Spirit for applying it with power to my soul, and for revealing it with such vivid distinctness to my mind.. . . I was then confirmed in my former faith and hope. I was perfected in love. Perfect love had cast out all the previous fear that had given me so much torment.[4]

- It was the Lord's work. He perfected it, without the aid of anyone . . . I have long prayed for confirmation in my hope, and he has graciously granted it. I now know, not from nature and the Bible alone, that there is a God in Israel. The evidence is in my heart.[5]

- I am a redeemed, saved sinner, trusting alone in Jesus for salvation. I have ceased to look into myself for anything to commend me to God. I turn away from everything but Christ, and set him always before my face. I labor to promote his cause with my feeble instrumentality; but there is no merit in it; it is done as a servant. I have had no conflicts since; because I have ceased to look at self. I look at none but Jesus. He is able and willing to save me, and I have given my soul into his hands.[6]

Response

7. Alexander Pope, an English poet wrote, "Hope springs eternal in the human breast." Do you agree with this statement? Why or why not?

_____
_____
_____
_____
_____

(Suggested reading – Deuteronomy 28:64-66; Psalm 30:7; Proverbs 13:12)

8. What are the practical consequences for a person who is living without hope?

_____
_____
_____
_____
_____

(Suggested reading – Judges 17:6; Isaiah 6:9-10; Acts 7:51)

9. Why do you believe so many people die without ever accepting Jesus Christ as Lord and Savior; particularly those who have plentiful access to the gospel message?

(Suggested reading – Isaiah 61:3; Jeremiah 29:11; Romans 8:6; 1 Thessalonians 5:8; Philippians 4:6-7)

10. How, if at all, does hope assist us in daily life on Earth?

(Suggested reading – Romans 8:37-39; 2 Corinthians 5:4-5; Hebrews 7:16-22)

11. How do believers know their living hope is guaranteed?

12. Will there ever be a time when living hope will no longer be required?

Practical Points to Consider

Unanswered or Additional Relevant Questions

Prayer

Heavenly Father, thank you for your love, mercy, and grace. Thank you for the hope you have given me through your Word, Son, and Holy Spirit. Lord, help me to remember that life on Earth is simply a dress rehearsal for eternity. Keep me mindful of the life-giving hope you placed within me and your desire for me to share that hope with everyone you place in my path. In Jesus's name I pray. Amen.

Journaling

A Living Hope – God's Gift of Encouragement

Lesson 12
Eternal Life – The Final Gift of Christmas

For the wages of sin is death, but the gift of God is eternal life in Christ Jesus our Lord. (Romans 6:23)

On the twelfth day of Christmas my true love gave to me, eternal life with him, my jubilee.

Observation

Twelve Gifts of Christmas, chapter 14, discusses the last gift of Christmas; eternal life with God the Father, Jesus the Son, and the Holy Spirit. This everlasting gift is the object of our living hope.

Eternity with the triune God is a reality for believers. Yet, how often do we truly meditate on this fact? Dwight L. Moody, also known as D. L. Moody (1837–1899), was an American evangelist who founded the Moody Bible Institute and Moody Publishers. In his book, *Heaven*, he writes:

> "A great many persons imagine that anything said about heaven is only a matter of speculation. They talk about heaven much as they would about the air. Now there would not have been so much in Scripture on this subject if God had wanted to leave the human race in darkness about it.. . . What the Bible says about heaven is just as true as what it says about everything else. The Bible is inspired. What we are taught about heaven could not have come to us in any other way than by inspiration. No one knew anything about it but God, and so if we want to find out anything about it, we have to turn to his Word.[1]

> There are men who say that there is no heaven. I was once talking with a man who said he thought there was nothing to justify us in believing in any other heaven than that we know here on Earth. If this is heaven, it is a very strange one—this world of sickness, sorrow, and sin. I pity from the depths of my heart the man or woman who has that idea. This world that some think is heaven, is the home of sin, a hospital of sorrow, a place that has nothing in it to satisfy the soul.[2]

I do not think that it is wrong for us to think and talk about heaven. I like to locate heaven, and find out all I can about it. I expect to live there through all eternity. If I were going to dwell in any place in this country, if I were going to make it my home, I would want to inquire about the place, about its climate, about the neighbors I would have, about everything, in fact, that I could learn concerning it.

If any of you were going to emigrate [leave one's own country to live elsewhere permanently], that would be the way you would feel. Well, we are all going to emigrate in a very little while to a country that is very far away. We are going to spend eternity in another world, a grand and glorious world where God reigns. Is it not natural, then, that we should look, listen, and try to find out who is already there, and what is the route to take?[3]

If there is anything that ought to make heaven near to Christians, it is knowing that God and all their loved ones will be there. What is it that makes home so attractive? Is it because we have a beautiful home . . . beautiful lawns . . . beautiful trees . . . beautiful paintings . . . beautiful furniture? Is that all that makes home so attractive and beautiful? Nay, it is the loved ones in it; it is the loved ones there.[4]

It has been said that there will be three things which will surprise us when we get to heaven—one, to find many whom we did not expect to find there; another, to find some not there whom we had expected; a third, and perhaps the greatest wonder—to find ourselves there."[5]

Contemplation

(Suggested reading – Revelation 1:1 & 3; 22:20)

1. How did the revelation come to John? What is its purpose?

(Suggested reading – Revelation 21:10 through 22:5)

2. What (not who) will we see in heaven?

(Suggested reading – Revelation 4:2-8; 5:6-11; 7:9 & 17; 21:3, 22 & 27)

3. Who will we see in heaven?

(Suggested reading – Revelation 7:16 & 21:4-25)

4. What (not who) will we not see or experience in heaven?

(Suggested reading – Revelation 20:15 & 22:15)

5. Who will not be in heaven?

(Suggested reading – Revelation 19:5 & 22:3)

6. What will we do in heaven?

_____

_____

_____

_____

Inspiration

Prodigal Ministries in Louisville, Kentucky provides housing for people, recently released from incarceration, who need a safe place to live as they transition back into society. Once a week the residents are offered a home-cooked meal followed by a Bible study. Pat and Ken, friends who operate this ministry, invited me to join this group. Once a month I would meet with these men to enjoy food, followed by a Bible study led by Tony, Win, and Jim. The only thing better than the food was the company.

Shortly before Christmas 2015, I was given the opportunity to lead a Bible study. The topic I chose (or so I thought) for that evening was "Christmas Gifts From Our Heavenly Father." As I was preparing the lesson, God used that study time to impress upon my mind a basic fact in a very powerful way: "Understand and appreciate how much I have done to save you." I had always known this, but had not meditated on it as often as I should have. Nor did I realize, at that time, all that God had done for me.

In the preface to this study guide I said, "I exhibited the faith to believe. I . . . I . . . I. Sometimes, I think it's all about me." God showed me through his Word that he provided me with the faith to believe in him. His Spirit was the originator of my faith; not me. Throughout the lesson preparation, God revealed more and more of what he has done to save me. Conversely, I realized how little I had contributed to his plan of salvation. The Holy Spirit gave me a deeper perspective of the cross; a lesson I will never forget as long as I have my mind. God, as he often does with his children; chastises the failure, corrects the weakness, and then blesses the repentant one. That Christmas Bible study in 2015 became the genesis of the book *Twelve Gifts of Christmas From our Heavenly Father* and this subsequent study guide.

God has, is, and will continue to be in the business of transforming sinful, wretched humans into his eternal heirs by his love through Jesus Christ and the indwelling Holy Spirit. Calvin W. Laufer (1874–1938) was a Presbyterian minister serving congregations in New York and New Jersey. In his book, *The Incomparable Christ*, he speaks about God's love and the transforming power of Jesus's blood writing:

> "The cross of Jesus Christ is the spiritual magnet of the world and is drawing to itself all mankind.. . . Wherein, then, lies the marvelous and irresistible power of the cross? How has this instrument of cruelty and death become the symbol of love and life? . . . The cross has this all-subduing, magnetic power; because it gives dramatic expression to eternal love. In the transcendent sacrifice of Jesus, the love of God is revealed."[6]

This entire study has been about God's plan to redeem fallen humans and the gifts he offered us to achieve that goal. This creates a sobering question in my mind. What, if anything, did I contribute to this plan? I am reminded of a man who, some 2,600 years ago, was sent by God into the middle of a valley full of dry, decaying bones. At God's command, the man spoke to the bones and then watched. The Lord brought the bones back to life and they became a vast army. Scripture tells us:

"Then he [God] said to me [Ezekiel]: 'Son of man, these bones are the people of Israel. They say, "Our bones are dried up and our hope is gone; we are cut off"'" (Ezekiel 37:11).

Those dry, dead bones in the valley represent my life without Christ. If I am perfectly candid, I did nothing, or very little, like those dead bones, to be resurrected. The simple truth is, I brought only three things to the foot of the cross:

- An acknowledgement of a desperate need for healing, which I knew was impossible for me to obtain on my own.
- A fallen, human nature that imprisoned me in the shackles of sin and death.
- A contrite heart, desiring to be brought back into right relationship with God.

The author has written elsewhere:

- "As the psalmist wrote, 'My sacrifice, O God, is a broken spirit; a broken and contrite heart you, God, will not despise' (Psalm 51:17). God didn't devise his plan of redemption and offer me these marvelous gifts because of how good or bad I am or how little or hard I try. God did these things for his name's sake; because he created and loves me. All he asks in return is for me to love him."[7]
- "So, I find myself where I began, sitting in my living room on Christmas morning staring through spiritual eyes at twelve brightly wrapped presents. Each has a tag inscribed in bold, blood-red letters, 'To Stan—from your Heavenly Father.' What shall I do with these gifts offered by God? Do I accept or reject them? Those are the only two choices for important decisions, particularly those having eternal implications. God will not force me to decide one way or the other.[8]

Response

7. What is the most beautiful place you have ever seen? What made it so?

(Suggested reading – Ephesians 1:4; 2 Timothy 1:9-10; 1 Peter 1:18-20)

8. When did God devise his plan for our salvation and eternal home?

9. What are some of the things you have on your "to do" or "to ask" list once you are in heaven?

10. What are some of the things about eternity that are most precious to you?

11. How does knowing the eternal, indescribable glory that awaits you, help you navigate daily life on Earth?

12. At the moment of your repentance, what did you bring to the foot of the cross?

Practical Points to Consider

Unanswered or Additional Relevant Questions

Prayer

Heavenly Father, thank you for your love, mercy, and grace. Thank you for your plan of salvation and the eternal home you have prepared for those who believe in Jesus Christ. I don't understand a love that great, but I accept it and thank you for it. Keep me mindful of how much you paid and how little I contributed to your plan of grace. Help me to remain grateful every day and recognize the opportunities you provide for me to share your message about the kingdom of heaven. It is in the name of your Son, my Lord and Savior, Jesus Christ that I pray. Amen.

Journaling

Twelve Gifts of Christmas - From Our Heavenly Father - Study Guide

Small Group Leader's Guide

Each lesson in this study relates to information contained in the book *Twelve Gifts of Christmas From Our Heavenly Father*. However, you don't need that book to use this guide. Each participant only needs their Bible, since each gift is a foundational topic in God's Word.

Citations are included at the end of this guide. No one should conclude from this study that God extends only twelve gifts to humanity. He extends every good and perfect gift (James 1:17); far more than a dozen.

Each lesson contains the following sections:

Observation

- "Observe the commands of the Lord your God, walking in obedience to him and revering him" (Deuteronomy 8:6).
- This section addresses the topic discussed in the book, *Twelve Gifts of Christmas*. This note is only there for those who have that book and may want to refer to it for additional information.

Contemplation

- "And we all, who with unveiled faces contemplate the Lord's glory, are being transformed into his image with ever-increasing glory, which comes from the Lord, who is the Spirit" (2 Corinthians 3:18).
- This section contains a set of questions on the topic to be considered in the light of Scripture.

Suggested Reading

- The "Contemplation" and "Response" sections contain the questions for each topic. When specific passages of the Bible are "suggested reading" for the participant, they are located with the question. Only a very few applicable verses related to the topic are "suggested reading." This is to provide a starting point for each person to begin their study, if they so desire. Each participant will likely find numerous additional, relevant passages that provide the answer to the question posed.

Inspiration

- "We remember before our God and Father your work produced by faith, your labor prompted by love, and your endurance inspired by hope in our Lord Jesus Christ" (1 Thessalonians 1:3)
- This section contains a brief story or statements leading us to consider how we will respond regarding the topic in question.

Response

- "Do not merely listen to the word, and so deceive yourselves. Do what it says" (James 1:22).
- This section contains a set of questions exploring our response on the topic.

Practical Points to Consider

- "How can a young person stay on the path of purity? By living according to your word.. . . I have hidden your word in my heart that I might not sin against you" (Psalm 119:9, 11).
- Here is a place to record learning points and applications derived from the study.

Unanswered or Additional Relevant Questions

- "Do not forsake wisdom, and she will protect you; love her, and she will watch over you. The beginning of wisdom is this: Get wisdom. Though it cost all you have, get understanding" (Proverbs 4:6-7).
- Here is a place to record any unanswered questions, additional questions, or topics that may warrant more in-depth study.

Prayer (Supplication)

- "May my supplication [request for help] come before you; deliver me according to your promise" (Psalm 119:170).
- Here is a short prayer giving thanks to our heavenly Father for his guidance on the topic at hand.

Journaling

- A place for your notes or thoughts on anything else related to the topic being discussed.

Hopefully, those who complete this study will:

- Realize how much God provided to each of us so we may be able to obtain eternal life with him one day.
- Understand how little we contributed to God's plan of salvation.
- Consider how these two facts should impact our lives from this day forward.

Small group leaders should feel free to make any adjustments to this material to tailor this study to the needs of your group. May you be richly rewarded for the time and effort spent studying God's Word on these important eternal matters.

Notes

Lesson 1 – Jesus Christ – The First Gift of Christmas

[1] Stanley Holstein, *Twelve Gifts of Christmas From Our Heavenly Father*, (Bluffton, OH: SLH Publishing, 2022); 7.

[2] George C. Lorimer, *The Galilean or Jesus the World's Savior*, (Boston: Silver Burdet, 1892); Pdf. https://www.loc.gov/item/33036812/; 17.

[3] Ibid., 414-415.

[4] M. G. Easton, *Illustrated Bible Dictionary and Treasury of Biblical History, Biography, Geography, Doctrine, and Literature*, "Christ," (New York: Harper & Brothers, 1893); 142-143.

[5] M. G. Easton, *Illustrated Bible Dictionary and Treasury of Biblical History, Biography, Geography, Doctrine, and Literature*, "Messiah," (New York: Harper & Brothers, 1893); 460–461.

Lesson 2 – Grace – The Gift of God's Plan

[1] Thomas Davidson, Editor; *Chambers' Twentieth Century Dictionary (Part 2 of 4: E-M)*, "Grace," (Urbana, Illinois: Project Gutenberg, 2012); www.gutenberg.org/ebooks/38538; 364-365.

[2] Rev. A. A. Benton, M.A., Editor; *The Church Cyclopaedia A Dictionary of Church Doctrine, History, Organization and Ritual*, "Grace," (Philadelphia: L. R. Hamersly & Co, 1884); https://ia800104.us.archive.org/31/items/churchcyclopdiad00bent/churchcyclopdiad00bent.pdf; 341.

[3] Robert N. McKaig, D. D., *The Life and Times of the Holy Spirit, Volume 1*, (Chicago and Boston: The Christian Witness Co., 1908); Pdf. https://tile.loc.gov/storage-services/service/gdc/dcmsiabooks/li/fe/ti/me/so/fh/ol/ys/00/mc/ka/lifetimesofholys00mcka/lifetimesofholys00mcka.pdf; 20-21.

[4] Stanley Holstein, *Twelve Gifts of Christmas From Our Heavenly Father*, (Bluffton, OH: SLH Publishing, 2022); 41-42.

[5] Alexander Patterson, *The Greater Life and Work of Christ as Revealed in Scripture, Man and Nature*, (New York, NY: Christian Alliance Publishing Co) 1898; posted by Library of Congress at https://babel.hathitrust.org/cgi/pt?id=loc.ark:/13960/t7zk6h49w&view=1up&seq=5; 128-129.

Lesson 3 – Life – A Daily Gift from God

[1] Stanley Holstein, *Twelve Gifts of Christmas From Our Heavenly Father*, (Bluffton, OH: SLH Publishing, 2022); 59.

[2] Michael J. Carlowicz, Lawrence Friedl, and Kevin A. Ward, *Earth*, (Washington, DC: National Aeronautics and Space Administration, 2018); https://earthobservatory.nasa.gov/ContentFeature/earth-book2019/downloads/249517_EARTH%20BOOK-TAGGED.pdf; 1.

[3] William Paley, *A View of the Evidences of Christianity*, (London, Printed by S. Hamilton, Weybridge, 1810); Pdf. https://www.loc.gov/item/33017064/; 36.

⁴ Rev. James B. Walker, D.D., *The Doctrine of the Holy Spirit, or, Philosophy of the Divine Operation in the Redemption of Man*, (Cincinnati: Jennings and Pye; New York: Eaton and Mains, 1901); Pdf. https://tile.loc.gov/storage-services/service/gdc/dcmsiabooks/do/ct/ri/ne/of/ho/ly/sp/00/wa/lk/doctrineofholysp00walk/doctrineofholysp00walk.pdf; 82-83.

⁵ Ibid., 130.

⁶ Ibid., 154.

Lesson 4 – Being Chosen by God Is His Gift

¹ Robert N. McKaig, D. D., *The Life and Times of the Holy Spirit*, (Chicago and Boston: The Christian Witness Co., 1908); https://tile.loc.gov/storage-services/service/gdc/dcmsiabooks/li/fe/ti/me/so/fh/ol/ys/00/mc/ka/lifetimesofholys00mcka/lifetimesofholys00mcka.pdf; 18-19.

² Stanley Holstein, *Hope Through the Truth, Standing in the Gap in America*, (Bluffton, OH: SLH Publishing, 2021); 122-123.

³ Hugh Price Hughes, M.A., *Essential Christianity*, (New York, Chicago, Toronto: Fleming H. Revell Company, 1894); Pdf. (https://tile.loc.gov/storage-services/service/gdc/dcmsiabooks/es/se/nt/ia/lc/hr/is/ti/00/hu/gh/essentialchristi00hugh/essentialchristi00hugh.pdf; 81-82.

Lesson 5 – Our Faith in God Comes From Him

¹ Stanley Holstein, *Twelve Gifts of Christmas From Our Heavenly Father*, (Bluffton, OH: SLH Publishing, 2022); 83-84.

² Rev. James B. Walker, D.D., *The Doctrine of the Holy Spirit, or, Philosophy of the Divine Operation in the Redemption of Man*, (Cincinnati: Jennings and Pye; New York: Eaton and Mains, 1901); Pdf. https://tile.loc.gov/storage-services/service/gdc/dcmsiabooks/do/ct/ri/ne/

of/ho/ly/sp/00/wa/lk/doctrineofholysp00walk/doctrineofholy-sp00walk.pdf; 98-99.

[3] Ibid., 102.

[4] Ibid., 123-124.

[5] Ibid., 155.

Lesson 6 – The Desire to Live for God Is His Gift

[1] Robert N. McKaig, D. D., *The Life and Times of the Holy Spirit*, (Chicago and Boston: The Christian Witness Co., 1908); https://tile.loc.gov/storage-services/service/gdc/dcmsiabooks/li/fe/ti/me/so/fh/ol/ys/00/mc/ka/lifetimesofholys00mcka/lifetimesofholys00mcka.pdf; 175.

[2] Ibid., 27.

[3] Ibid., 176-178.

Lesson 7 – The Holy Spirit – God's Power in Us

[1] Alexander Patterson, *The Greater Life and Work of Christ as Revealed in Scripture, Man and Nature*, (New York, NY: Christian Alliance Publishing Co., 1898); https://babel.hathitrust.org/cgi/pt?id=loc.ark:/13960/t7zk6h49w&view=1up&seq=5; 190-191.

[2] George B. Thompson, *The Ministry of the Spirit*, (Washington, D.C.: Review and Herald Publishing Assn, 1914); Pdf. https://tile.loc.gov/storage-services/service/gdc/dcmsiabooks/mi/ni/st/ry/of/sp/ir/it/00/th/om/ministryofspirit00thom/ministryofspirit00thom.pdf; 11.

[3] Steve Brantley and Bobbie Myers, US Geological Survey, "Mount St. Helens – From the 1980 Eruption to 2000," US Geological Survey, March 1, 2005, https://pubs.usgs.gov/fs/2000/fs036–00/.

[4] National Museum of the United States Air Force, "Fat Man Atomic Bomb," https://www.nationalmuseum.af.mil/Visit/Museum-Exhibits/Fact-Sheets/Display/Article/196220/fat-man-atomic-bomb/.

⁵ George B. Thompson, *The Ministry of the Spirit*, (Washington, D.C.: Review and Herald Publishing Assn, 1914); Pdf. https://tile.loc.gov/storage-services/service/gdc/dcmsiabooks/mi/ni/st/ry/of/sp/ir/it/00/th/om/ministryofspirit00thom/ministryofspirit00thom.pdf; 25.

⁶ Ibid., 17-18.

⁷ Ibid., 58-59.

Lesson 8 – The Fruit of the Holy Spirit – God Producing in Us

¹ George B. Thompson, *The Ministry of the Spirit*, (Washington, D.C.: Review and Herald Publishing Assn, 1914); Pdf. https://tile.loc.gov/storage-services/service/gdc/dcmsiabooks/mi/ni/st/ry/of/sp/ir/it/00/th/om/ministryofspirit00thom/ministryofspirit00thom.pdf; 7-8.

² Robert N. McKaig, D. D., *The Life and Times of the Holy Spirit*, (Chicago and Boston: The Christian Witness Co., 1908); https://tile.loc.gov/storage-services/service/gdc/dcmsiabooks/li/fe/ti/me/so/fh/ol/ys/00/mc/ka/lifetimesofholys00mcka/lifetimesofholys00mcka.pdf; 189.

³ George B. Thompson, *The Ministry of the Spirit*, (Washington, D.C.: Review and Herald Publishing Assn, 1914); Pdf. https://tile.loc.gov/storage-services/service/gdc/dcmsiabooks/mi/ni/st/ry/of/sp/ir/it/00/th/om/ministryofspirit00thom/ministryofspirit00thom.pdf; 203-204.

Lesson 9 – The Word of God – His Gift of Revelation

¹ Laurence W. Scott, *The Great Crisis in the Life of Christ His Trials and Crucifixion*, (Cincinnati: F. L. Rowe, 1909); https://tile.loc.gov/storage-services/service/gdc/dcmsiabooks/gr/ea/tc/ri/si/si/nl/if/00/sc/ot/greatcrisisinlif00scot/greatcrisisinlif00scot.pdf; 7.

² Ibid., 9-10.

³ Ibid., 11.

⁴ Ibid., 12-13.

[5] Ibid., 17, 19.

[6] Henry M. Morris, *The Genesis Record A Scientific and Devotional Commentary on the Book of Beginnings*, (Grand Rapids, MI: Baker Book House, 1976); 17.

[7] Ibid., 21-22.

[8] Ibid., 22.

Lesson 10 – Adopted by God – His Gift to Spiritual Orphans

[1] George C. Lorimer, *The Galilean or Jesus the World's Savior*, (Boston: Silver Burdet, 1892); Pdf. https://www.loc.gov/item/33036812/; 145.

[2] American Tract Society, *The Gift of the Knees: or The Ministry of Prayer, the Ministry of Power*, (Astor Place, NY: Hurd and Houghton, 1872); Pdf. https://tile.loc.gov/storage-services/service/gdc/dcmsiabooks/gi/ft/of/kn/ee/so/rm/in/00/un/se/giftofkneesormin00unse/giftofkneesormin00unse.pdf; 5.

[3] Ibid., 5-6.

[4] Paul Sabatier, Louise Seymour Houghton, translator; *Life of St. Francis Of Assisi*, (London: Hodder & Stoughton, 1919); https://www.gutenberg.org/; 12.

[5] U.S. Department of Health and Human Services, Children's Bureau, "Trends in Foster Care and Adoption: FY 2010 – FY 2019," https://www.acf.hhs.gov/sites/default/files/documents/cb/trends_fostercare_adoption_10thru19.pdf.

Lesson 11 – A Living Hope – God's Gift of Encouragement

[1] Alexander Pope, Esq., *An Essay on Man; in Four Epistles*, (Hartford: Silas Andrus, 1824); https://ia903408.us.archive.org/12/items/essayonman01pope/essayonman01pope.pdf; 13.

[2] Stanley Holstein, *Hope Through the Truth, Standing in the Gap in America*, (Bluffton, OH: SLH Publishing, 2021); 166-167.

[3] H. E. Taliaferro, *The Grace of God Magnified: An Experimental Tract*, (Charleston: South Western Baptist Publication Society, 1857); https://www.loc.gov/item/unk82033249/; 18-19.

[4] Ibid., 86-87.

[5] Ibid., 109.

[6] Ibid., 122.

Lesson 12 – Eternal Life – The Final Gift of Christmas

[1] Dwight L. Moody, *Heaven: Where It Is, Its Inhabitants, and How to Get There*, (Chicago: F. H. Revell, 1885); https://www.loc.gov/item/unk82039720/; 7.

[2] Ibid., 11.

[3] Ibid., 15.

[4] Ibid., 27-28.

[5] Ibid., 29.

[6] Calvin Weiss Laufer, *The Incomparable Christ*, (New York, Cincinnati: The Abingdon Press, 1915); Pdf. https://tile.loc.gov/storage-services/service/gdc/dcmsiabooks/in/co/mp/ar/ab/le/ch/ri/00/la/uf/_1/incomparablechri00lauf_1/incomparablechri00lauf_1.pdf; 199-201.

[7] Stanley Holstein, *Twelve Gifts of Christmas From Our Heavenly Father*, (Bluffton, OH: SLH Publishing, 2022); 197-198.

[8] Ibid., 195.

Other Books By This Author

Available at Barnes & Noble.com and other online book stores.

www.ingramcontent.com/pod-product-compliance
Lightning Source LLC
Chambersburg PA
CBHW021103080526
44587CB00010B/366